Go to Work *and*
Take Your Faith Too!

Go to Work *and* Take Your Faith Too!

Ross West

PEAKE ROAD
Macon, GA

ISBN 1-57312-094-4

Go to Work and Take Your Faith Too!

Ross West

Peake Road
6316 Peake Road
Macon, Georgia 31210-3960
1-800-747-3016

Biblical quotations, unless otherwise noted, are from the
New Revised Standard Version of the Bible (NRSV).

The paper used in this publication
meets the minimum requirements of
American National Standard for Information Sciences—
Permanence of Paper for Printed Library Materials.
ANSI Z39.48–1984

Library of Congress Cataloging-in-Publication

West, Ross, 1943–
    Go to work and take your faith too! / Ross West.
    x + 166 pp.   6" x 9" (15 x 23 cm.)
    Includes bibliographical references.
    ISBN 1-57312-094-4   (alk. paper)
    1. Work—Religious aspects—Christianity.
    2. West, Ross, 1943–
    I. Title.
    BT738.5.W47   1997
    248.8'8—dc20   97-38534
                                                          CIP

Contents

Preface vii

Faith and the Workplace

Chapter 1
What Does Faith Have to Do with Daily Work, Anyway?.........................1

Chapter 2
Work: Curse, Blessing, or . . .? 17

Chapter 3
Can Faith Really Be Lived at Work?...35

How to Relate Daily Work to Faith

Chapter 4
Find and Follow Your Personal Purpose in Life 47

Chapter 5
Live By Faith's Values 59

Chapter 6
Look for Faith's Meaning in Daily Work 79

Chapter 7
Relate to Fellow Workers as a Person of Faith..89

Chapter 8
Choose How You Balance Life 103

Chapter 9
Lighten Up 125

Chapter 10
Practice Personal Disciplines for Integrating Work with Faith 131

How Churches Can Help

Chapter 11
How Churches Can Help 149

Conclusion 159

Select Bibliography..161

About the Author 165

Preface

What, if anything, does religious faith have to do with daily work? This is the question I began asking myself a few years ago. I made it more personal by forcing myself to ask what was uniquely Christian about *my* approach to the work I was doing each day. As I pondered these questions from a general and a personal standpoint, I came to the conclusion that Christians and churches have had too little to say about a Christian approach to work. Worse, many of us have given too little thought and even less action to answering our questions concerning it.

My own religious tradition tended to give these answers: Being Christian at work means (1) telling others at work about your faith, (2) being honest and ethical, and (3) giving a full day's work for a full day's pay. The emphasis seemed to be that your true Christian service did not occur when you were at work but rather when you were (1) on the grounds of the church building and (2) engaged in activities of worship, religious education, or committee meetings, if you were truly faithful.

Understand, I'm for the numbered answers in the preceding paragraph (though I confess I'm not very fond of committee meetings). Still, these answers seemed entirely too limited in scope to be as broad as it seemed to me that faith ought to be if it truly spoke to all of life. What kind of faith left out a third of a person's life, the time spent at work, as if work had no substantial meaning in itself?

Asking these questions wouldn't have been so bad if one discounted the kind of work I was doing at the time. I had been a pastor of churches for ten years and then involved in my denomination's publishing enterprise for nearly a dozen more years when I began asking these kinds of questions. I *did* find meaning in my work, but not as much as I could have wished and not as often as I might have hoped. This particular publishing enterprise occasionally demonstrated the worst characteristics of a bureaucracy. So I found myself living in this bureaucratic environment, much like millions of other workers in other than Christian institutions.

Out of my experience of searching, I wrote my first book, *How to Be Happier in the Job You Sometimes Can't Stand.* That book and the seminars I conducted on its theme seem to have helped a good many people deal with the realities of modern work. Since then, I've moved out of the work of religious publishing into the broader field of publishing, writing, leading seminars, and consulting with businesses as well as churches.

I didn't make a career change because I didn't like religious publishing. I'm glad to have had significant roles in developing Bible
study materials for millions of people in my denomination and in other
Christian churches. I even liked being a pastor. But opportunities in
these areas were not available at a significant point in my life when I
felt I needed to make a change, and so I found myself moving in
another direction. As I moved out of the kind of work generally identified as religious, I did so with both regret and a strong measure of
assurance from my faith that this move was the right one.

My new, secular role outside of "religious work" has forced me to
ask even more pointedly the question of how one's faith ought to relate
to one's daily work, if indeed it should at all. I no longer have the
luxury of hiding behind the thought that I'm engaged in religious publishing, and so of course my work is related to my Christian faith.

Like the vast majority of people of faith, I now live in a working
world that sometimes seems fairly far removed from where I worship.
So how does my faith relate to my work, and does it at all or enough?
Is it even possible to live my faith in the work itself—not just away
from that work or during the coffee breaks or mealtimes of that work?

I have written this book in the midst of the everyday struggles of
the workplace. The workplace with which I am familiar through
experience or observation is a place where . . .

• Dollars count and have to be accounted for.
• Goals are set and must be met.
• Bosses look over your shoulder and sometimes pound on your head
  or other parts of your anatomy.
• People face tough ethical choices, sometimes between doing the right
  thing or keeping their jobs.
• The maze of bureaucracy has to be navigated.
• Charges of sexual harassment and racial discrimination are made and
  sometimes dealt with and sometimes not.
• People are concerned about children, but are torn because they have
  to let someone else care for them when they're sick or hurt.
• People get angry, gossip, backbite, and sometimes get fired.
• Other people get the promotion you wanted.
• Workers do tasks that seem meaningless and useless but that have to
  be done because that's just the way the work is structured or because
  the boss's boss's boss wants it done, with no other explanation.
• The company does things you question.
• Today can seem remarkably like yesterday and much like you
  anticipate the coming day to be as well.

But there's another side to this place. The workplace is where . . .

• Significant lifelong friendships are made and nourished.
• People who share few things in common reach out to help make good things happen for people they don't know and may never see.
• Work that everybody can be proud of gets done and gets done well.
• People get the financial resources for living, making downpayments on dreams, and supporting families where children need food and clothing.

. . . It's a good place.

I described the workplace with which I am familiar so you would know that I did not write this book from the sidelines or from high up in an ivory tower looking down. Speaking of ivory towers, I have two theological degrees, one of them a Doctor of Ministry degree in Biblical Studies. Because, however, of my participation in the everyday world of work, I approach the subject of meaning in work on the level with every other person of faith seeking to understand how—and whether—the world of work relates to the realm of faith.

Through my thinking, reading, and living, I've arrived at some answers that are satisfying enough to me, at least until I learn better ones. I hope these answers can be helpful to you. I also hope they will contribute to the continuing dialogue that needs to take place among people of faith about how we spend a third of our lives. The fact is, individual people of faith have not in many cases thought long enough and hard enough about how they relate their faith to their work—or need to. They certainly may not have taken enough action in relating their faith to their work.

You see, I find it difficult in many cases to determine who of my work associates is a person of faith after all. Making that determination is not my job, of course; I gladly leave it to God. Perhaps, too, observers might wonder the same thing about me. The reality is, though, discerning the difference faith makes in people's lives at work is not easy or obvious. Most people of faith seem to do an excellent job not practicing their "piety before others in order to be seen by them" (Matt 6:1). The problem now may be that some of us have taken that concern a little too far. We're careful not to practice our piety much of anywhere except the church property, if there. Furthermore, even the people at work who speak the loudest about being religious may act least like people of faith. There's too big a gap between profession and practice in the lives of individuals.

At least as damning is that the vast majority of churches have listened too little to the voices of people in the world of work. In her book, *In the Age of the Smart Machine: The Future of Work and Power,* Shoshana Zuboff, a researcher on the effects of technology on the world of work, wrote that she learned through her research that people have a lot to say about their work, but that few people are willing to listen. The church is a part of the vast potential audience that needs to learn to listen to people express their struggles, joys, and hopes from the world of work.

I confess that when I first started thinking about this whole area of living faith in the world of work, I thought of myself as a bit like Elijah when he was all alone in a cave, believing he was the only prophet left who was faithful to God. You may recall that in a still, small voice, the Lord assured Elijah that there were plenty of other faithful people left, not just him (see 2 Kgs 19). That's what I've found, too.

As I've shared my pilgrimage in conversations, seminars, and sermons, I've discovered I have plenty of company. Lots of fellow strugglers are concerned about this matter of living faith in the world of work and are doing something about it. They may not dot their *i*'s alike, or even use the familiar words of faith, but their words, actions, and struggles reflect the depth of their spiritual concern. You will meet some of them in this book, and this book may lead you to think of others whom you know.

There aren't enough of us yet, though, and we're not yet making enough impact—far from it. So there's plenty of room for you to live your faith where you are, including at your place of work. If you will, you'll probably find others who are interested in such a life, too. Come on along. You'll find the journey exhilarating, and you'll find fellow pilgrims heading the same direction.

Chapter 1
What Does Faith Have to Do with Daily Work, Anyway?

"What place," I asked the thirtyish businessperson, "does your faith have in your work?" Though I had met Randy only the day before, I decided to ask him that question when I saw him silently bowing his head—in prayer, I presumed—in a public place as we prepared to eat a meal.

Both us were participating in a business seminar that in all appearances had little or no direct relevance to what most people would call faith. It was all business. Beyond Randy's action of bowing his head, I had seen nothing that would distinguish him as a person of faith any more than anyone else at the seminar, including me. Neither he nor I nor any of the rest of the seminar participants from across the nation had engaged in any actions that readily would have identified us as people of faith as far as I could tell. Probably others there were indeed people of faith; some likely were not.

All of us—women and men—were behaving as decent, courteous human beings. Even though that sort of behavior is sometimes unusual in itself, it doesn't necessarily indicate that one is a person of faith. It may just indicate that one has good manners. Mind you, I believe that good manners generally are better than bad manners. But faith is about more than good manners, isn't it?

My new friend replied to my question about faith's relation to work with this rhetorical question, "Well, we've not heard anything about faith in this conference, have we?" I listened, nodded, and waited for further comments.

"My experience," he continued, "is that faith has no place in business." His attitude indicated that he wished it did, and that he was speaking of the environment in which he worked rather than about his own intent. I inquired about what he meant.

He explained: "Sometimes after I've taught Sunday School and attended church on Sunday, I think about the coming day at work. And I wonder, what in the world does what I've just done here at church have to do with anything I have to do at work this coming week?"

I indicated that I heard and understood. I then commented that my current role had enabled me to see this whole matter of faith and daily work from a different perspective than I had as a pastor or denominational employee. I readily agreed that the world as viewed from the world was a different world from the world as viewed from the place of worship.

"Now you see what we laypeople are up against, don't you?" he commented, with feeling. I had to agree that I did.

My friend and I and many others were struggling with this question: What does faith have to do with daily work, anyway? The answers that come from the faith side of this question have been scarce, especially when heard from the work side of life. Even the answers that have been forthcoming have been generalizations mainly, much easier to say than to figure out how to put into practice. These twin problems make answering the question in a pointed and specific manner an important, even crucial, undertaking.

A Personal Question

What part of your life and mine do you think God cares about? Part of it or all of it? Most likely, you answer, as do I, "Why, all of it, of course."

We've been taught that God is present everywhere. So, we have little trouble assuming that this understanding of God means that God is present at our place of work even as God is present at our place of worship.

But do we really believe that God is present at and in our work? Actually believing that God is present when we are working is quite another matter for many of us a great deal of the time. Acting on that belief is even more difficult. In spite of the platitudes we may hear, think, and say on Sunday, the world of business on Monday seems to be a world apart from the place and time of worship.

While worship may or may not be an other-worldly experience for us, we're quite certain that business is very much a this-worldly experience, often far removed from our general understanding of the life of faith. A great many workers, including people of faith, would probably consider their work to be much closer to hell than to heaven, in fact.

A Personal, Perhaps Inconsequential, Perspective

When I was in the process of moving from my work in a denominational publishing house to a place of work in the broader world, a friend of mine mentioned something puzzling to me. What he said became abundantly clear later, however.

My friend is a retired missionary whose career also included a stint in a secular organization in between times of service as a

missionary in another culture. He graciously assured me of his su̶
and his belief that good things would happen for me in my new v̶
ture. I gladly accepted his encouragement, especially since I ha̶
grown to feel a kinship with him and valued his opinions.

Then he made the mysterious statement. After his words of
encouragement, he continued, "You'll soon find out you won't be able
to talk to your present friends anymore, though."

"What the heck could he mean?" I wondered to myself. And so,
my disbelief showing, I said to him, "Why's that?"

"Well, you won't be able to talk to them because you won't even
use the same language," he continued. Now that I think about it, I
believe I saw a twinkle in his eyes when he said that.

"Oh?" I asked with further disbelief, since my language skills have
been fairly good, and I figured they would continue to be, even if I
were moving to Texas.

"You'll see," he said knowingly and mysteriously.

"Darn," I thought to myself. Indeed, though, I soon saw; actually, I
heard.

I can give you a clue about what I heard by telling you another
story. When I served as a pastor in a small town, each time I entered
the barbershop, the barber in the first chair would greet me in a loud
voice, "Hello, *Preacher.*" He put an unmistakable over-emphasis on the
word "preacher." His voice was loud enough that not only the men in
the barbershop but also the women in the beauty shop next door could
hear him, too. A moment of hushed silence in both places followed
before the conversation picked up again.

Somehow I had the feeling that neither the women nor the men
were praying in that moment of silence. I could see the men; I knew
they weren't praying. They stared straight ahead, faces aglow. Whatever it was on their faces, it wasn't prayer. I assumed the women in the
beauty shop were having a similar experience.

It did not take me long to figure out that the loud greeting was not
a sign of honor and the moment of silence was not a sign of reverence.
These occurrences were meant to serve one purpose: to alert everyone
to watch what they said since the "man of God" was now present. But,
if you're a layperson, you knew that long before I did, didn't you?

I often wondered about the conversation I had missed. Now I know
for sure what I earlier only suspected. I don't wonder any longer.

No one calls me "Preacher" anymore, you see. So, at work in the
business world I'm now a part of all types of conversations that
include plenty of four-letter words I formerly did not hear when my

nited and those with whom I talked were fore-
·ful in their speech. Understand, the vocabulary
Thanks to the people I grew up with plus vari-
I've not had to ask someone to explain what a
rd meant. But I'd just not been hearing these
round of life as a pastor and then in religious

The use of language is a simple illustration of the chasm that generally exists between the world of work and the life of faith. My own
background and inclinations still lead me to choose different language
from that of some of my business associates to express my views.
However, I hereby assure my business friends—women as well as
men—that they do not need to clean up their language for my benefit.
I accept my associates and appreciate them as they are, even though I
choose to use other language with which to express my ideas, frustrations, and joys. (My closest friends in the business world know I'm
telling the truth about the entirety of the preceding sentence!) Still, the
contrast between the language used at work and the language used at
church—depending on your church as well as your place of work, of
course—is often quite great.

Moreover, and more seriously, even as I adopt this generous attitude toward the language of too many people in too many workplaces,
this statement in Ephesians 5:4 reminds me that one can be too generous: "Entirely out of place is obscene, silly, and vulgar talk; but
instead, let there be thanksgiving." The context of this verse suggests
that this statement may have particular reference to the sort of lewd
joking about sexual matters that is sometimes heard in conversations in
the business world.

Interestingly, that sort of speech is now being curtailed, or at least
guarded more closely, in the work world. The cause is not, however, so
much that people are exercising their faith, but more that such talk can
be the basis of sexual harassment charges, lawsuits, and the resulting
payout of big dollars by companies and individuals. The same indictment can be made concerning comments and jokes that demean people
of other races. The fact is people of faith themselves utter too many
hurtful words under the guise—read, "deceit"—of humor.

William E. Diehl, formerly a top executive for Bethlehem Steel
and now a management consultant and author, evaluated the impact of
the Christian faith in his own business world in this manner by saying
that religion did not seem to him to play much of a role in the lives of
people in business.[1] The friend I met at the business seminar merely
echoed Diehl's evaluation.

You may find this evaluation harsh. Diehl further observes, however, that during his more than three decades of work experience he heard little conversation from his associates about matters of faith. Talk about religion was simply not a part of corporate culture, even if he had been inclined to talk about it himself.[2]

For all the obviousness of four-letter words in the workplace and all the lack of conversation about religion there, I'm concerned about considerably more than these matters as I ask what does faith have to do with work, anyway. Let's probe this question further.

The Great Divide

This question—what does faith have to do with work?—itself suggests a compartmentalization of life. Compartmentalization in this case means the notion that our faith can exist in one compartment and our work can exist in another, with little or no touching or interchange between the two.

Such a schizophrenic approach to faith and work is unfortunately widespread. More than one person of faith seeks to live as if life at the office or factory is untouched by life at worship, and vice versa. Attempts to live in such a manner put a person squarely in line with the current trend of modern society, unfortunately.

Robert Bellah is a sociologist who with his associates researched the mind-set of adults in the United States regarding the relationship between public and private life.[3] He observed,

> The most distinctive aspect of twentieth-century American society is the division of life into a number of separate functional sectors: home and workplace, work and leisure, white collar and blue collar, public and private.[4]

The trend, then, is against joining a variety of separate compartments in our lives, including those of faith and work. Faith is relegated to the compartment labeled "private," work is put into the compartment labeled "public," and never the twain meet—or at least only rarely.

One person illustrated the problem by saying that when he went to church, no one seemed particularly interested in what he did at work. Moreover, when he went to work, no one seemed particularly interested in what he did at church or even whether he went.

The chasm runs deep and wide. The chasm is particularly obvious to someone who has lived on both sides of it, and it's also obvious to those who have to commute at least weekly from one side to the other.

It may not be as obvious to those who live only on one side of it, such as professional church leaders.

But why does the chasm exist? It exists because, as presently structured, the world of work operates from a different understanding of at least three areas important to faith. Those three areas are values, meaning, and relationships.

Consider the first area—values. Could it be that the values deemed important to business and those considered important to faith are exclusive to each other? Consider and perhaps list on a piece of paper your answers to these questions:

What words characterize business?
What words characterize faith?
Are the words on each list different or the same?

Could it be true, as scholar Susan Brooks Thistlethwaite suggests, that business values "competition, independence, assertiveness" and that these values are not "the core values of Christianity"?[5] Anecdotal and experiential evidence confirm that business does indeed value "competition, independence, assertiveness." Indeed, to challenge such values would appear to many in our culture to be challenging our entire way of life.

Concerning competition, Coach Lombardi's famous statement, "Winning isn't everything; it's the only thing," is held up as the model for go-getters at work and everywhere else. This, in spite of the fact that Lombardi himself later appears to have expressed regret that he had said it, or at least that it had been taken to mean that people should disregard human values.[6] Furthermore, no less a figure in business than management expert W. Edwards Deming has condemned the practice of competition among employees, saying it is detrimental to real achievement.[7]

The value of independence is ingrained in our heritage. Individuals, families, businesses, and groups are encouraged to "stand on their own two feet." The positive features of this emphasis often are distorted quite handily with the unspoken addition, "without regard for anyone else."

The third value of business, assertiveness, begins at least with the advice given a child to "stand up for yourself." The emphasis continues into adulthood, with books touting the value of assertiveness and training even being given in it. I cannot help but think of someone's quip about assertiveness training, suggesting that we imagine what all the world will be like when we all have assertiveness training! I've caught glimpses of it in traffic jams in Dallas, Atlanta, New York, and other cities, and, believe me, it's not a pretty sight.

On the other hand, what would be the core values of Christianity? One way of answering this challenging question is to recall Jesus' reply to the question of which commandment was the first of all. Remember? He said,

> The first is, "Hear, O Israel: the Lord our God, the Lord is one; you shall love the Lord your God with all your heart, and with all your soul, and with all your mind, and with all your strength." The second is this, "You shall love your neighbor as yourself."(Mark 12:29-30)

Recall, too, that Paul identified love as greater than various areas of human striving and exalted it above faith and hope (1 Cor 13). If loving concern for others is basic to the Christian faith, and if various expressions of self-interest are basic to business, the conflict is apparent. At the risk of oversimplifying the issue, perhaps we can say that faith emphasizes the power of love while the world of work emphasizes and operates on the love of power, if we define power broadly to include economic power as well as besting and even dominating others.

Another reason for the depth and breadth of the chasm is the way business and faith approach the matter of meaning in life. Bluntly put, business tends to see the bottom line—the accumulation of wealth for corporations and individuals—as the measure of meaning. Even though such accumulation of wealth need not come at the price of dishonesty, the bottom line for business's idea of meaning is still the bottom line, by and large.

Few businesses these days, for example, would deal with the problem of a no-longer competent employee as one manager did a few years ago. The manager had the task of finding a way to deal with a person who had been employed in his job for twenty years but who really was not qualified for it. The manager had inherited the problem. The man's hiring in that particular job was the company's mistake. At the same time, though, the manager was responsible for getting the best production out of his unit. What was he to do as both a business executive and a person of faith? Should the values of his faith even enter into consideration?

The manager struggled with the matter until finally he and his superiors decided that the best thing was to move the man to a job he could do but to continue to pay him at his current higher rate of pay. Therefore, the company got the opportunity to move a more able person into the job but was still able to preserve benefits for the man, though not his sense of esteem.[8]

Admittedly, employment law makes this incident tricky. Still, to what extent would the solution be acceptable to top management and stockholders today? To what extent would concern for the person involved even be considered?

The fact that many readers will consider this action unusual is a way of demonstrating the point about business's meaning being attached to the bottom line. The manager's actions were not the ordinary way of approaching the problem. We find it difficult to picture a business operating in such a manner.

If work in general is such a frustrating, meaningless pursuit, then why do we spend our hours, days, and years in such a manner? Many reasons come into play, of course, but workers—including people of faith—find themselves operating at the lower levels of meaning in relation to their work. Put more simply, they work to get the money needed for living. In such cases, although their work provides them bread—and bread is certainly important, even necessary—their work provides them only bread.

Still, they—and we—know the deep-down truth of the biblical statement that we do not live by bread alone (Matt 4:4). Rabbi Harold Kushner states it this way: "We work for meaning as much as for money. We work so that our days will not be empty of meaning."[9] But we wish there were more meaning in those days, don't we? Moreover, we believe there ought to be.

This belief puts us in conflict with the prevailing views of our culture about work, however. This conflict can be illustrated in how our culture views vocations that focus on helping people but receive little monetary reward for the effort. The culture gives lip service to the importance of such vocations. It does not actually value them, though, by rewarding them with the standard currency that indicates value in our culture, namely dollars and status.[10]

So, the divide between working only for money or for money and too little meaning becomes a great gulf. We participate in business's quest for the bottom line because the bottom line is important to us, too, as we attempt to support ourselves and others. We still believe, however, that there's more to life than the bottom line.

This concern about the scarcity of meaning was important in driving me to consider this whole matter of faith and work, in fact. I suspect it's a concern of yours as well. We want our work to have meaning in itself and not be *only* a way to get something else.

We know that the "something else" is important, of course. Still, we yearn for our work to be more of a goal in itself and not just a means. A key question we'd like to answer in a manner that satisfies us is the one posed by authors McMakin and Dyer: "What gives my life meaning, and how can I incorporate that in my vocation?"[11] The ideal life would be for us to be able to demonstrate fully in our daily work the meaning that is important to us.

The importance of community, of human relationships, is a third area on which business and faith seem to differ. In theory, and certainly at times and places in practice, business affirms the importance of community, of building and enhancing positive relationships on the job as well as off the job.

The general reality is often quite different, however. One psychologist who studies and treats business executives under stress suggests that the traits that make a person successful in business actually operate to undermine relationships on and off the job. He cites the focus of business on goals to the exclusion of the process for achieving them—and relationships are at the heart of the process. The second and third deadly traits that make a person successful in business but unsuccessful in relationships—and, indeed, in life in general—are lack of time and refusal to admit weakness.[12]

Tom Chappell, president of Tom's of Maine, identifies the matter of relationships as crucial in his dawning realization of what was bothering him about how his company was operating. He had founded the company a dozen years earlier, and the company had become so successful, it was moving beyond its original market and to a significantly higher level of success. Something bothered Chappell about what was happening, though. It bothered him so much, he went to Harvard Divinity School to try to find what it was.

Chappell found the answer as his professor lectured on the ideas of the Jewish philosopher Martin Buber. Buber suggested that relationships tend to be "I-It," meaning we expect something in return from the other person, or "I-Thou," meaning we relate to people on the basis of respect and even love, and that attitude is not based on whether we hope to receive anything back from the relationship. We simply relate to people in the "I-Thou" manner because that is the way we are to relate to people, who are valuable in themselves and not just for what they can do for us.

When Chappell encountered these ideas, he realized that he and his company's managers tended to operate on an "I-It" basis, treating people as objects, even though his faith taught him that "I-Thou" was the appropriate way to relate to people.[13] This is the difference in a nutshell about how business and faith differ in how each considers relationships with people.

The film *Regarding Henry* illustrates well the difficulties of having real relationships at work. Harrison Ford stars as Henry, a hard-driving, ultra-successful attorney in a prestigious New York law firm. Henry is a taker, the ultimate picture of greed. He cuts corners, and he wins big cases and big money as a result. Henry's colleagues admire and applaud him. Indeed, they are in awe of him.

Henry lives in a huge Manhattan apartment. He has a beautiful wife who once loved him but now loves mainly the life he provides for her since he has little time for her. They have a brilliant twelve-year-old daughter who hates Henry because he ignores her and who feels terribly pressured by the demands for success her parents put on her.

One night Henry runs out of cigarettes. What happens to Henry is a good example of how bad for one's health smoking can be. He goes to the small grocery next door to get a pack of cigarettes. He comes in at the wrong time on the wrong customer. A robbery is taking place. Soon, Henry is shot—twice. His life hangs by a thread.

The rest of the film is the story of Henry's discovery of the poverty of his life, including his work life. Except for the young woman attorney who is having an affair with him, no one at the office really cares about him very much except as a moneymaker for the firm.

During Henry's recovery, his coworkers make some clumsy attempts at kindness, but these efforts don't go very far. The relationship of Henry and his coworkers is revealed to be based, at bottom, on the profit motive, even though one can sense in Henry's coworkers the uneasy feeling that something within their humanity wishes it were different.

In real life, doesn't everyone who both works and senses at least a glimmer of humanity within himself or herself wish it were different at work, too? Sometimes business leaders speak of "our family here at work." However well-intentioned such a remark is, the likelihood of it being true is rather small. Not today, anyway. The downsizings—uh, sorry, rightsizings—in business in the past few years have made suspect such comments as "our family here at work." Family members do not kick fellow family members out of the house when the going gets tough. Businesses do this on a regular basis, though.

The point of these comments is not whether such actions are demanded by business strategies based on economic realities. Rather, the point is, finding genuine community at work has never been easy and is becoming more and more difficult today.

Furthermore, competition for promotions and recognition tends to discourage employees from building the kind of self-giving relationships that characterize *koinonia,* the genuine community that ought to exist in human relationships bound together by a common faith.

The employee at the lowest level in the organization and the executive at the highest level would do well to evaluate the price they may be paying as human beings for their position in the organization, day in and day out. Doing business while ignoring or shortchanging the business of living is an unwise tradeoff. But it's one many people of faith confront every day they go to work.

The Tragedy of the Division

The compartmentalization of faith and work leads to tragedy for all concerned. Every individual or entity involved loses. The individual, the world of work, and the church—they all lose.

Individual employees who are people of faith lose when they are at work. They lose there because they spend a third of their lives isolated from the values, meaning, and patterns of relationship their faith has taught them to hold dear and practice.

Such a schizophrenic way of life cannot be good, can it? It's not good for our consciences when we act in ways contrary to our values and explain it away by saying, "That's business." It can't be good for our sense of self, our souls themselves, when we try to exist in a poverty of meaning for eight or more hours every day. It can't be good for our common humanity when we must engage continually in relationships that are similar to the relationships between people and things, or even between things and things. Human beings are made for relationship. To deprive ourselves of truly human relationships wounds our spirits.

Individual employees also lose when they are at their place of worship. They may hear challenges there to become better, more faithful disciples. But the challenges often imply that such discipleship is to be expressed by and large within the four walls of the church or through involvement in church activities. The message communicated is, participation in such activities plus adherence to conventional middle-class morality defines Christianity.

This sort of message leaves many people of faith wondering about—and maybe questioning inwardly or outwardly—whether a faith that ignores a third of their lives is really a faith worth having or at least of doing very much about. How can worshipers integrate the faith to which they are called in worship with the life they live the rest of the week? They are the same people, but they may find little recognition of this fact. So the individual person of faith loses because of the chasm that separates the world of faith and the world of work.

The world of work also loses. One observer of the worlds of work and faith, John C. Haughey, suggests:

> One of the major causes of workplace alienation, sloppy work, and underinvestment in work on the part of many otherwise religious people is that they have not seen or been taught the connection between daily work and God's intentions in making us.[14]

The chasm between the world of work and the world of faith creates among modern Christians a kind of monasticism that isolates them from the activities of the larger society without encouraging them to offer to that society the unique and needed resources of faith. As a result, the world of work is deprived of the leavening influence of faith's values, meaning, and sense of community. Individualistic self-enhancement rules the world of work by default as well as by design when people of faith avoid demonstrating their faith on and through their jobs.

The world of faith loses as well. The community of faith needs the regular challenges from the world of work to remind it that real faith is made flesh in life, including the life that occurs in the world of work.

Religious leaders sometimes appear to communicate that attending the congregation's activities is the highest mark of faith. Such faithfulness is not unimportant and may well deserve commendation. But the world of faith as seen in such activities is too small a world for a living faith. Living faith overflows the channels of congregational activities and spills over into all of one's world. Quaker philosopher and theologian Elton Trueblood warned prophetically of thinking that the Christian cause made progress mainly on the weekends. Instead, he suggested that what Christians did during the week might be far more important than what they did on Sundays.[15]

Another observer of and participant in the world of faith gave an even more severe indictment. Pierre Teilhard de Chardin, a French Catholic theologian, wrote:

> The great objection brought against Christianity in our time, and the real source of the distrust which insulates entire blocks of humanity from the influence of the Church . . . is the suspicion that our religion makes its followers inhuman.[16]

Inhuman? I can't think of a more serious charge about religion than that it makes its followers inhuman. What could the theologian have meant? I take the statement to mean that we people of faith somehow appear to others to be living in a world of unreality. We evidently seem to be ethereal spirits with only a touch of body here and there (well, more here than there, of course), as if there were something sinful in itself about being human and participating in the affairs of everyday life.

If that's how we people of faith really are, then we have failed to grasp the implications of the Bible for everyday life. The wisdom literature of the Bible, for example, is concerned with how to get along best in the world—*this* world. Proverbs contains much practical advice about work, including this bit of wisdom: "One who is slack in work is close kin to a vandal" (18:9).

Too, Israel's prophets would not let the nation's leaders believe they had performed their duty to God when they engaged in worship activities without a concern for justice in daily life, including the world of business. Jeremiah, for example, proclaimed:

> Woe to him who builds his house by unrighteousness, and his upper rooms by injustice; who makes his neighbors work for nothing, and does not give them their wages. (22:13)

Moreover, the message of the New Testament is based on the incarnation, the belief that "the Word became flesh and lived among us" (John 1:14) in the daily affairs of life. The New Testament proclaims the incarnation as the means by which we know God most clearly and most fully. One implication of this idea is that people of faith can and should experience God in the dailiness of life, including the world of work.

The Importance of Bridge Building

People who live near rivers understand the importance of bridges. My first official pastorate was at a small church in a community located on the Ohio River. The waters of the river lapped at the fields of the farmers who attended the church, in fact. The nearest bridge across the river was sixty miles away. We could see Indiana on the other side of the river, but we couldn't get to it. When at last a bridge was built nearby, another world was opened to that small community.

More and better bridges are needed between the world of faith and the world of work. Indeed, the world of faith and the world of work can be the same world. Theologian and philosopher Elton Trueblood put it succinctly and plainly when he wrote, "The way in which we grow potatoes is as much a matter of God's will as is the way in which we pray or sing."[17]

The fact is, however, people of faith likely do not recognize this truth in practice to the extent needed to enrich their lives, not to mention to enrich the worlds of work and faith. But that's not God's fault. Rather, as Haughey has observed, "It is a sign of poor religious education and the superficiality of our discernment."[18] Both the church and people of faith themselves bear responsibility for their shortcomings in relating faith and work.

Further, both the church and individual people of faith bear responsibility for correcting the problem. Even further, all entities involved—people of faith, the church, and the world of work—stand to benefit to the extent that faith's values, meaning, and community can be made present and practiced in the world of work.

So what's needed? Nothing less than rediscovering, reaffirming, and reshaping for this day a focus on how living faith relates to the world of daily work.

More than a half-century ago and in the context of a world threatened by war, Dietrich Bonhoeffer, a prominent German Lutheran theologian, wrote: "It is becoming clearer every day that the most urgent problem besetting our Church is this: How can we live the Christian life in the modern world?"[19] More than a half-century later, we still don't have a satisfying answer.

The situation today is different and at least outwardly less dramatic than that in which Bonhoeffer lived. The question is still the same: *How can we live the Christian life in the modern world—including the world of work?*

Notes

[1]William E. Diehl, *In Search of Faithfulness: Lessons from the Christian Community* (Philadelphia: Fortress Press, 1987) 5.

[2]Ibid., 5, 7.

[3]Robert N. Bellah et. al., *Habits of the Heart: Individualism and Commitment in American Life* (Berkeley CA: University of California Press, 1985) viii.

[4]Ibid., 43.

[5]Susan Brooks Thistlethwaite, "Interpreting Faith and Work Through Gender," in Stephen Hart and David A. Krueger, *Faith and Work: Personal Needs and Congregational Responses,* The Center for Ethics and Corporate Policy's Congregations and Business Life Project, final report (Chicago: The Center for Ethics and Corporate Policy, 1991) 57.

[6]Alfie Kohn, *No Contest: The Case Against Competition,* rev. ed. (Boston: Houghton Mifflin Co., 1992) 3, 248.

[7]Ibid., 240, citing comments by W. Edwards Deming in a videotape series, "The Deming Library."

[8]William E. Diehl, *Christianity and Real Life* (Philadelphia: Fortress Press, 1976) 73-75.

[9]Harold Kushner, *When All You've Ever Wanted Isn't Enough* (New York: Pocket Books, 1986) 150.

[10]Robert S. Michaelson, "Work and Vocation in American Industrial Society," *Work and Vocation: A Christian Discussion,* John Oliver Nelson, ed. (New York: Harper & Brothers, 1954) 153.

[11]Jacqueline McMakin with Sonya Dyer, *Working from the Heart* (San Diego CA: LuraMedia, 1989) 25.

[12]Reported in Ellyn E. Spragins, "High Level Anxiety," *Working Woman* (March 1993): 58.

[13]Tom Chappell, *The Soul of a Business: Managing for Profit and the Common Good* (New York: Bantam Books, 1993) 12-13.

[14]John C. Haughey, *Converting Nine to Five: A Spirituality of Daily Work* (New York: Crossroad, 1989), 33.

[15]Elton Trueblood, *Your Other Vocation* (New York: Harper & Brothers, 1952) 57.

[16]Pierre Teilhard de Chardin, *The Divine Milieu: An Essay on the Interior Life* (New York: Harper & Row, 1960) 68.

[17]Trueblood, 64.

[18]Haughey, 60.

[19]Dietrich Bonhoeffer, *The Cost of Discipleship* (New York: Macmillan, 1963) 60.

Chapter 2
Work: Curse, Blessing, or . . .?

As I drive to work in the morning, I sometimes glance into the faces of other drivers and the passengers in their cars. Because of the time of day and the normal patterns of life, I presume almost everyone of us is headed for work. I must say I don't see many smiles. We're a haggard bunch, by and large.

The early hour may be one reason for the scarcity of even semi-happy faces, and the pressure of driving in traffic may be another. I suspect, however, that a larger component of the evident lack of enthusiasm for the day has to do with the likelihood that many are headed for a day in which they wish they could be doing something other than what awaits them at work.

I further reason that surely some of the faces I see were in a place of worship the past week or will be in one the next week. Identifying who was and who wasn't and who will be and who won't be is not possible from the looks on their faces, however—and not even from the way they drive, I might add, but that's another matter!

Only a bumper sticker here or there offers a distinguishing clue, and such symbols are no guarantees of the commitments of the drivers and passengers. If the car ahead of you has on its bumper a sticker that invites, "Honk if you love Jesus," you would not be wise to accept the invitation at the moment a red light changes to green. I might say, too, that I tend to wonder about the drivers of those cars that have the sign of the fish, representing Christianity, on the trunk but also have a radar detector on the dash.

Nevertheless, assuming that at least some of the people I see as I drive to work are people of faith, I find myself asking what work means to them. What ideas do they hold about work? What does their faith teach them about work?

Through the centuries, faith has taught more than one view of the subject of work. In this chapter, I intend to summarize those views as identified in the Bible. Now, I'm aware that my statement of intention will turn some people on because Bible study is especially meaningful to them or because they hunger to know what the Bible teaches on this subject as well as perhaps on other subjects. Because I've spent a good number of years developing skills in interpreting the Bible, even to the point of being able to read the Greek New Testament, turning to the Bible for direction comes readily to mind; it's second nature for me.

Maybe that's not you, though. If so, as if you need it, then you have my permission to skip this chapter. I do believe, however, if you'll read or even skim this chapter, you'll pick up some insights you need about the biblical view of work. Furthermore, becoming aware of the multiplicity of views will help you broaden and deepen your perspective on work. Such a broadened and deepened perspective might also lead you and other people of faith to greater inner satisfaction with work if not to more smiles on the way to work. The intent is to provide help in relating faith to daily work and seeing particularly how faith can express itself in daily work.

Work as Divine Assignment

We can trace the idea of work as God's assignment to human beings to the first chapters of the first book of the Bible. One reference to this assignment can be seen in God's instructions to human beings to

> be fruitful and multiply, and fill the earth and subdue it; and have dominion over the fish of the sea and over the birds of the air and over every living thing that moves upon the earth. (Gen 1:28)

The order to "be fruitful and multiply, and fill the earth" surely relates to the function of extending the human family. The population—*over*population—of our world is evidence that human beings have outdone themselves in obeying this instruction!

The instructions to "subdue" and "have dominion" can be understood as relating to the idea of work. Of course, the intent of these instructions may be simply to give the powerful message that human beings are to be caretakers of the world on God's behalf as creatures made in God's image. It is also possible, however, to understand that the instructions to "subdue" and "have dominion" involve functioning, working, on God's behalf in developing the world God brought forth out of chaos. Genesis 2:2 understands God to be a working God who "rested on the seventh day from all the work that he had done." This working God is the God in whose image human beings are made. As creatures made in this working God's image, human beings have been assigned the task of working on God's behalf in the midst of God's creation to subdue and have dominion over it.

The creation account in Genesis 2 amplifies and personalizes God's assignment to human beings to work: "The Lord God took the man and put him in the garden of Eden to till it and keep it" (v. 15). God had planted this garden and placed the man in it (v. 8). Note that as with the creation account in Genesis 1, the creation account in

Genesis 2 pictures God as having worked and then as having assigned to human beings the responsibility for working to care for what God had planted. This assignment means that we have a role in God's plan for developing the world, and we fulfill that role when we work.

Illustrations of this view can be seen in specific places in the Bible. For example, Exodus 35:30-35 identifies God as the source of the skill Bezel and Ahola used in working with gold, silver, brass, and cloth, as well as other kinds of work. Such abilities were useful in constructing the tabernacle and its furnishings. Similarly, Isaiah 28:23-29 refers to God as the source of the farmer's creativity in growing crops. Each of these illustrations implies that God is intimately involved in daily work and that the worker is participating with God in developing the world.

The divinely-assigned nature of work for Christians can be seen pointedly in Colossians 3:23-24. The message in these verses is directed particularly to slaves. Even though they are slaves, they are to do their work in recognition that God, not human beings, is their ultimate master. As they work, they are to work for the Lord, not for their earthly masters.

Work, then, is our divine assignment to develop our world on God's behalf. Furthermore, work is the means by which we carry out that assignment.

We may wonder, of course, to what extent the specific daily work we do really contributes to developing the world of which God has made us caretakers. We do have choices to make as to which part of the garden we work in, and it seems reasonable to assume that we would be more productive in certain areas than in others. The overarching truth, however, is still the same. Our daily work is, at least potentially, a way to carry out God's assignment to human beings made in the early chapters of Genesis.

Work was a divine assignment before work was ever viewed as a curse. Even in the paradise of Eden, work was a part of life and considered to be an assignment by God.

Paul affirmed this idea of work in his letters to the Thessalonian Christians, especially the second letter. To some of their company who evidently felt themselves above the need to work, Paul pointedly said,

> Anyone unwilling to work should not eat. For we hear that some of you are living in idleness, mere busybodies, not doing any work. Now such persons we command and exhort in the Lord Jesus Christ to do their work quietly and to earn their own living. (2 Thess 3: 10-13)

Work as Curse

The idea of work as curse comes from an interpretation of God's pronouncement to the erring man in Genesis 3. The man and the woman had yielded to the trickery of the serpent and eaten the forbidden fruit. God then gave to each—serpent, woman, and man—a punishment appropriate to their respective roles.

The nature of the punishment on the serpent, the woman, and the man provides answers to questions about each of them. Why does the serpent crawl on its belly, having no legs, and why metaphorically does the deceitfulness of evil so readily attack human beings? Why is woman's way of childbearing so difficult and her relationship with man so conflicted? Why is man's work of tilling the soil so hard and unproductive? The punishments meted out provide answers to these questions.

The curse on the ground is the specific source of the idea of work as curse or punishment. "Cursed is the ground because of you; in toil you shall eat of it all the days of your life" (v. 17). Note the parallels in this punishment on the man to the punishment on the woman. As the woman is now in a contradictory, conflicted relationship with the man from which she was created (vv. 21-23), so also the man is now in a contradictory, conflicted relationship with the very ground from which he himself was created. Alienation, estrangement, discord, and difficulty now mark these relationships that once were characterized by unity and intimacy.

But is the curse on the ground the source of work? Not at all, for we have already noted that work existed in Eden even prior to the temptation, the yielding, the discovery, and the punishment. So, the result of the curse on the ground is not that work itself becomes a curse. Rather, the result is that now work, as commentator Gerhard von Rad describes so picturesquely,

> makes life so wretched, that it is so threatened by failures and wastes of time and often enough comes to nothing, that its actual result usually has no relation to the effort expended.[1]

As another biblical commentator, C. U. Wolf, summarizes more succinctly, "Sin did not make labor necessary, but it made it less rewarding and subject to frustrations and problems."[2] Genesis 3 thus suggests that the wrong choice of the man and the woman changed them as well as their circumstances. Therefore, work becomes drudgery.

The prospects for finding meaning and satisfaction in daily work seem rather dismal then, don't they? In a similar light, a parishioner who had just heard the pastor speak about the terrible consequences of the Fall is supposed to have remarked, "Well, if it's as bad as all that, then God help us." Of course, that's just the point of the rest of the biblical story.

God did not leave human beings in the predicament described in Genesis 3:16-19. God's provision of redemptive grace can remove at least some of the consequences of life in a world gone astray from God. Work's frustrations and problems are among the consequences with which God's grace can assist if not remove entirely.

Then why is work so frustrating and not at all a paradise even if we are people of faith? One way of answering this question is to realize that even God's grace does not return people to the paradise that existed prior to the Fall. Rather, following the biblical image, we continue to live in a fallen world where the consequences of sin are evident. That world includes the world of work.

Even so, we need not see work as being under a curse or a curse in itself. Rather, as theologian Dorothy Soelle affirms, "When God, incarnate in Jesus, became a worker, our understanding of work was finally freed from the tradition of the curse."[3] Jesus the carpenter demonstrated in his own life the redemption of daily work. So work itself is not a curse, however we may feel about our work on a given Monday morning.

Work as an Ordinary, Expected Part of Life

Work generally is portrayed with little fanfare in the Bible. Work is simply pictured as an expected, ordinary part of life. It is an integral part of the way life is. People work.

Adam keeps the Garden of Eden (Gen 2:15). Abel keeps flocks (Gen 4:2). Cain tills the ground (Gen 4:2). Jubal plays musical instruments (Gen 4:21). Tubal-cain forges instruments of bronze and iron (Gen 4:22). Rebekah draws water (Gen 24:16). Nehemiah is cupbearer to the king of Persia (Neh 1:11). Amos herds sheep and tends sycamore trees (Amos 7:14). The ideal woman works with her hands, provides food for her household, and engages in commerce (Prov 31:10-31). Peter, Andrew, James, and John fish (Matt 4:18-21). Luke is a physician (Col 4:14). Lydia sells purple fabric (Acts 16:14). Aquila, Priscilla, and Paul make tents (Acts 18:3).

Psalm 104 provides further evidence of the ordinary, expected nature of work. The psalm sings the greatness of God's creation, describing how various parts of it have their own unique place and fulfill their own special role. Birds build nests, goats live in high mountains, the sun sets, animals creep about by night, and lions seek their food during the day and sleep at night. The psalm concludes its lyrical recitation of how God's creation goes about its days and nights with these words we might not ordinarily consider lilting: "People go out to their work and to their labor until the evening."

The implication is that each of the activities mentioned in the psalm is as ordinary, as expected, as the other. The work of human beings is merely one of these activities. Thus, people's work is as much a part of the way life is as are any of the rest of the activities of God's creation.

The ordinary activities of daily work are a part of the background texture of the Bible. The images of shepherds tending sheep, fishermen going out to fish, farmers going out to sow—these are simply a part of the canvas on which biblical events and truths are portrayed.

The Bible spends little time debating whether or not work itself is good, bad, or indifferent. Work just is. Work is an expected, ordinary part of life.

Indeed, the idea of people *not* working is scandalous, an affront to what being a person of faith means. Paul taught this idea clearly in his letter to the Thessalonian church. In 1 Thessalonians 4:11-12 (see also 5:14), he affirmed the expected role of work when he encouraged the Thessalonian Christians

> to aspire to live quietly, to mind your own affairs, and to work with your hands, as we directed you, so that you may behave properly toward outsiders and be dependent on no one.

In Paul's second letter to the Thessalonian church, Paul admonished any who fail to see the expected nature of work and thus refuse to work: "For even when we were with you, we gave you this command: Anyone unwilling to work should not eat" (2 Thess 3:10). He cited his own behavior in working for his own support even though he had the right as a missionary and teacher to receive the support of the church (3:7-10).

Paul wrote to the Thessalonians that he worked for his own support in order to provide an example to them. If one were capable, working to support oneself was simply expected of people of faith. Any other course was scandalous and unacceptable.

A biblical proverb states in a positive manner a similar truth about the relationship between work and sustenance. Proverbs 16:26

observes: "The appetite of workers works for them; their hunger urges them on."

Working is the norm, the expected, the ordinary. Idleness is not only unusual, but unacceptable in a person of faith who has the capability to work.

Work as Worthy of God's Praise and Blessing

A number of passages in the Bible depict work as being worthy of God's praise and blessing. The book of Genesis tells how Isaac "sowed seed in that land, and in the same year reaped a hundredfold" (26:12). The latter part of the verse gives this crystal-clear evaluation: "The Lord blessed him." Later, God rewarded Joseph's labor on behalf of Potiphar, an officer of Pharaoh (39:5), and still later on behalf of Pharaoh himself (41:53-57; 45:6-8).

Exodus 31:1-11 identifies God as the giver of various skills to be used in work. He filled Bezalel

> with divine spirit, with ability, intelligence, and knowledge in every kind of craft, to devise artistic designs, to work in gold, silver, and bronze, in cutting stones for setting, and in carving wood, in every kind of craft. (vv. 3-4)

Bezalel's skills, along with those of Oholiab, were to be employed in building the tent of meeting, its furnishings, and the priestly garments and other elements used in the worship of God.

Psalm 107:36-38 also describes God's blessings on honest work. "They sow fields, and plant vineyards, and get a fruitful yield. By his blessing they multiply greatly, and he does not let their cattle decrease."

Deuteronomic theology carefully pointed out that as unfaithfulness to God resulted in retribution, so faithfulness to God meant blessings on the people, including on the people's labor.

> Blessed shall you be in the city, and blessed shall you be in the field. Blessed shall be the fruit of your womb, the fruit of your ground, and the fruit of your livestock, both the increase of your cattle and the issue of your flock. (Deut 28:3-4)

This view is evident not just in the book of Deuteronomy, but also in other books of the Bible whose message was shaped by this same perspective.

The wisdom literature of the Bible also affirmed the praiseworthy nature of work. Proverbs 31:10-31 praises the work of "a capable wife." Proverbs 22:29 praises the work of a skilled workman, asserting that he will have a place of honor. Such a worker would serve royalty, not common people.

The virtue of industriousness is praised in Proverbs 6:6-11. These verses praise the wisdom the ant exemplifies by its labor, in contrast to the foolishness the lazy person shows in his idleness. Proverbs 10:4 also praises diligent work, indicating that such work will be rewarded materially. Proverbs 21:5 echoes a similar message.

Proverbs 26:13-15 humorously condemns laziness and, by implication, praises industriousness in work. Verse 13 laughs at the lazy person who appears to say, "I can't go to work today. There's a lion in the street." Verse 14 pictures the lazy person turning over in bed, refusing to go to work. Verse 15 gives the ultimate picture of laziness. The lazy person picks up food to eat, but is too lazy to bring it back to his mouth!

Although the perspective of the book of Ecclesiastes is more negative than other wisdom writings, it also warns of the consequences of laziness (10:18) and thus affirms the blessings that come from work. In addition, Ecclesiastes repeats several times the praiseworthy nature of work in human life. "So I saw that there is nothing better than that all should enjoy their work, for that is their lot" (3:22; see also 2:24; 3:12-13; 5:18; 8:15; 9:7-9).

Ecclesiastes' seemingly positive view of work is really not so positive as it appears, however, for the book also speaks of the futility of work (3:9). The message of Ecclesiastes about work seems basically to be that since finding satisfaction in life is impossible and results in futility, then one had best seek satisfaction in the ordinary daily activities of life—eating, drinking, family relationships, and, yes, work. So even Ecclesiastes considers work to be a blessing, though admittedly in a subdued, resigned kind of way.

The root idea of work as blessing is this: God has structured work at its best in such a way that we can see, rejoice in, and be proud of the results of our labors. This is the ideal, and most workers would feel more positively about their work if they could experience this side of work more often.

Work as an Area of God's Concern

Although people may go through their days and nights at work as if God were somehow not interested, God indeed cares about the world of work. Specifically, God cares about the person in the world of work.

Indeed, the most important event in Israel's history, the Exodus, has its roots in God's concern for the oppression of God's people at work.

Exodus 1:13-14 records:

> The Egyptians became ruthless in imposing tasks on the Israelites, and made their lives bitter with hard service in mortar and brick and in every kind of field labor. They were ruthless in all the tasks that they imposed on them.

The next chapter records God's response to the people's "groaning" under their oppression: "God heard their groaning, and God remembered his covenant with Abraham, Isaac, and Jacob. God looked upon the Israelites, and God took notice of them" (2:24). Succeeding chapters in Exodus tell how God showed concern for their working conditions and acted on their behalf.

Leviticus 19:13 reveals another aspect of God's concern: "You shall not keep for yourself the wages of a laborer until morning." Deuteronomy 24:14-15 echoes and expands this concern for the laborer.

Other indications of God's concern for justice in the world of work can be seen in passages such as Proverbs 11:1: "A false balance is an abomination to the Lord, but an accurate weight is his delight."

The writings of the prophets likewise are filled with demands for justice in everyday life, which includes the world of work. These concerns can be summarized thus: "Let justice roll down like waters and righteousness like an everflowing stream" (Amos 5:24). Isaiah 58:3 speaks pointedly to the matter of justice in the world of work, charging, "Look, you serve your own interest on your fast day, and oppress all your workers."

Concern for the person in the world of work is evident in the New Testament as well. The person at work deserves to receive fair pay for work (see Luke 10:7). Further, working conditions—even of slaves— was a matter of concern for the community of faith. To masters of slaves came the warning, "Stop threatening them, for you know that both of you have the same Master in heaven, and with him there is no partiality" (Eph 6:9). God doesn't look at people's status in the world of work—whether slave or master, hourly employee or CEO—to decide whether God will be fair to them. God is every bit as concerned about the hourly worker as about the CEO.

The Bible also calls for a proper attitude in and toward work. The passage just referred to in Ephesians calls for obedient and enthusiastic service on the part of slaves. They are enjoined to serve their masters as if they were serving God (Eph 6:5-8; see also Col 3:22–4:1; 1 Tim 6:1; 1 Pet 2:18-25). One can only imagine how hard a task for slaves that must have been.

Not just attitudes but specific actions are also included in God's concern for the world of work. Titus 2:9-10 calls on slaves to refrain from backtalk and stealing. Paul's letter to Philemon encouraged him to accept the slave Onesimus as "more than a slave, a beloved brother," which perhaps was Paul's opening argument in calling for Onesimus's release from slavery (Philem 16). Paul commanded work, saying, "Thieves must give up stealing; rather let them labor and work honestly with their own hands, so as to have something to share with the needy" (Eph 4:28). The thief is to work rather than steal. Note the motive: to be able to give generously to the needy. They are to become truly honest Robin Hoods—working, not stealing, in order to give to the poor.

John the Baptist's heated message to the people of his day included specific instruction for the world of work (Luke 3:10-14). He instructed tax collectors to collect no more than authorized. He told soldiers, "Do not extort money from anyone by threats or false accusation, and be satisfied with your wages" (v. 14).

Work as a Limited Experience

For all the Bible's concern about work, the Bible also depicts work as a limited experience. Several biblical themes support this idea. First and foremost, the institution and observance of the Sabbath was a way of saying that work should be limited in nature. It's unfortunate that this fundamental truth about the Sabbath has been obscured in our society by the legal attempts to restrict Sunday activities and the legalistic approach to what should and shouldn't be done on Sunday.[4] In contrast, the Scriptures emphasize the humanitarian concern behind the Sabbath. Exodus 23:12 records the commandment to work six days and rest on the seventh. This "rest" is for people, animals, slaves, and aliens. The intended result is that all would be "refreshed." Deuteronomy 5:12-15 describes the Sabbath law in similar terms.

In addition, other passages emphasize the priority that worship takes over work. Leviticus 23 gives instructions about the three major annual celebrations in Israelite life. In each case, cessation of work on the Sabbath in order to worship is called for (vv. 7, 25, 36).

Exodus 34:21 reinforces the need for limiting work in order to gain rest and refreshment. It contends that the Sabbath law is to be obeyed "even in plowing time and in harvest time." In other words, being extraordinarily busy is no excuse for not limiting work in favor of rest.

Of course, we live in a society that never stops, not even for the Sabbath, whether one's religious tradition celebrates it on Friday, Saturday, or Sunday. This does not mean that people of faith do not need times and places for somehow making a statement with their lives in accord with the meaning of the Sabbath. We need a time for limiting work, for resting, and for thus recognizing that the world's values do not deserve our full allegiance.

Psalm 127:1-2 likewise puts a person's work in proper perspective. One's labor will not accomplish the desired goals without the Lord's help. In fact, working long and hard—from "can 'til can't"—is foolish, empty, and unproductive. Relying on the Lord is more important than feverish work without trust in Him. The foolishness of the tower of Babel may also illustrate a similar truth (Gen 11:4-8).

Further, Jesus' invitation to fishermen to leave their livelihood and come with him to "fish for people" teaches that work sometimes may need to be limited, too (see Mark 1:16-20). A higher purpose may take precedence over the daily tasks that appear to need to be done and over the job, career, or profession in which one is engaged.

Work as Calling and Vocation

Is work a "calling"? Is one "called" into certain kinds of work? Many church members believe so. A recent survey found that 40 percent of church members consider themselves to be "called" to their work. That figure increases to 46 percent among people who attend church weekly.[5] Even so, answering such questions about being "called" into one's work depends crucially on how one defines and understands the word "calling."

Sociologist Robert Bellah contrasts work as job, career, and calling. He suggests that job identifies work as "a way of making money and making a living."[6] Further, describing work as a career implies the idea of making progress and advancing in one's occupation. More powerful than either of these for Bellah, however, is the idea of work as calling. Bellah explains:

> In the strongest sense of a "calling," work constitutes a practical ideal of activity and character that makes a person's work morally inseparable from his or her life. It subsumes the self into a community of disciplined practice and sound judgment whose activity has meaning and value in itself, not just in the output or profit that results from it. But the calling not only links a person to her or her

fellow workers. A calling links a person to the larger community, a whole in which the calling of each is a contribution to the good of all.[7]

Bellah further states: "The absence of a sense of calling means an absence of a sense of moral meaning."[8]

The Protestant Reformers would have agreed with the importance Bellah places on seeing work as calling. Reformation theology accepted Christian calling as involving occupation in the world as well as service in the church on behalf of the gospel. Luther and Calvin promoted this idea. The Puritans, with their Calvinist theology, continued this line of thought as well.[9]

But, for all its serviceability as an idea, and in spite of the high percentage of churchgoers who see their work as a calling, is it really appropriate to apply the word "calling" to one's work? What biblical evidence is there for work as calling?

Here's a factor that deserves serious consideration: Though work skills may and should be used in the service of God, Scripture provides no specific instance of a person being "called" into what is ordinarily understood as a secular occupation.

In the Greek New Testament, the word for "to call" is *kalein.* Search the uses in the New Testament of this Greek word *kalein* and its noun forms, and no reference to calling to specific occupations of the day will be found. In the New Testament, the idea of being called refers only to being called to follow Christ (see Rom 8:30; 1 Cor 1:9) and, within that call, to serve Christ in carrying out his mission.[10] Where the Greek word for "to call" is used with theological significance in the New Testament and not merely to mean, for example, "to name" or "to invite" to an event, it "is a technical term for the process of salvation."[11]

Only in one instance in the New Testament—1 Corinthians 7:20—can the noun form *klasis* be construed to refer to a secular idea of "calling." Luther used this passage in constructing his doctrine of secular calling and vocation. More likely, in this instance, the word means "state"[12] or "condition." At any rate, the word in context cannot mean "vocation" in the sense of work since the reference is to the condition or state of the individual's life in general. The word refers most directly in the context in 1 Corinthians to the conditions of circumcision or uncircumcision as examples of states in life. As with the verb form *kalein,* the noun *klasis* is used almost without exception to refer to the call to salvation.[13]

Within the calling to follow Christ, of course, the Christian should use the skills and opportunities God provides. Paul used his skills as a tentmaker in order to provide a living for himself as he ministered as an apostle. Was Paul's work as a tentmaker a "calling"? No, not insofar as calling is understood as being a specific assignment to a given occupation. Yes, insofar as one understands calling to represent the overall thrust of Paul's life in response to God. With this view, Paul's work as a tentmaker is not in itself a calling but rather a useful way of enabling Paul to fulfill his calling as a Christian.

Paul described himself as being called to be an apostle (Rom 1:1); he did not describe himself as being called to be a tentmaker.[14] Paul's calling as an apostle and his occupation as a tentmaker were related in that his occupation as a tentmaker contributed to his calling as an apostle.[15] Unfortunately, however, this way of viewing occupation and calling does not provide enough help in the quest to find ways to see meaning in occupation. Rather, it seems to maintain the division between the two rather than helping to see how calling can be expressed in one's daily occupation.

Emory University professor James Fowler's pioneering work in the area of faith development provides help in seeing how faith applies to daily work. Fowler uses the word *vocation* in a way that is significantly similar to the scriptural understanding of calling. As we have seen, the derivation of calling is Greek. The derivation of vocation is Latin. The meaning of each respectively is closely related, however.

Fowler sets the stage for his explanation of the word vocation by first stating that our vocation is not our job, our occupation, our profession, or our career. He then asks:

> What is vocation then? I propose the following characterization: *Vocation is the response a person makes with his or her total self to the address of God and to the calling to partnership.* The shaping of vocation as total response of the self to the address of God involves the orchestration of our leisure, our relationships, our work, our private life, our public life, and of the resources we steward, so as to put it all at the disposal of God's purposes in the services of God and the neighbor.[16]

In this statement, Fowler is fully in line with the New Testament understanding of the idea of calling.

Is your work, whatever it is, a calling, then? Well, not according to the Bible. The idea is definitely on the right track, but the word is not the best choice. Your work is not in itself your calling. Your calling is to be a Christian. Your work, however, may well be—or can be—an *expression* of your calling to be a person of faith. Your daily work can be a means by which you seek to act day by day in partnership with God's purposes. Your daily work can be a vital expression of your vocation, your calling. Indeed, you must find ways to make it so if you are serious about your calling.

Okay, I confess that this distinction between your vocation as a calling or as an expression of your calling to be a person of faith may seem to be merely a quibble over theological words. Why bother? The distinction is valuable for at least two reasons.

First, making this distinction leaves room for people of faith to find various occupational expressions of their calling as they move through life. Thus, one may sense at a given point in life that a certain occupation or job is right and indeed the best available opportunity, but at another point in life move in a different direction. It's not that the earlier choice was a bad one and the later choice was a good one, but rather that each expression of calling has its place. Indeed, the earlier expressions generally contribute to and enhance the later ones.

The word "calling" is especially inadequate for the work situations in which so many are finding themselves today. Though I take a different approach to understanding the relation of our work to our faith, I am in agreement with theologian Miroslav Volf as he suggests:

> Modern societies . . . are dynamic. A single, permanent, salaried, and full-time form of employment has given way to multiple and frequently changing jobs. Such a dynamic society requires a dynamic understanding of work.
>
> It was clear to me that the dead hand of "vocation" needed to be lifted from the Christian idea of work. It is both inapplicable to modern societies and theologically inadequate.[17]

A second reason for distinguishing between one's calling to be a Christian and one's work is this: Making this distinction helps in recognizing that expressing our calling as people of faith involves more than work. In fact, it potentially involves every aspect of our lives. Retirement activities can be as much a part of one's calling as can work activities. So can recreational activities. Too, it helps people of faith who are out of work to recognize that they still have a calling. They are called to be Christians and are to find ways to express that calling, perhaps most immediately in finding a job that allows them to live out their faith.

Here's how I suggest you envision this idea of calling: Think of your calling to be a person of faith as a circle, and make it the largest circle. Inside the large circle place in smaller circles the other elements of your life—work, family, church involvement, community involvement, and so on. These activities and emphases thus become ways in which you express your all-important calling to serve God. They become your missions.

Work as Mission

A better word than calling to express one's intent to live out one's faith in one's work is this: mission. Rather than ask about whether Christians are *called* to their secular jobs, I suggest it's more appropriate to ask, "Are Christians *sent* to their secular jobs?" In other words, are they to be on mission there?

The answer to this question is a resounding yes. Laypeople are to be every bit on mission in their secular jobs as professional clergy are to be in their work. Understanding work as mission provides a way for connecting our work with our faith. It also helps to maintain the most appropriate use of the biblical word "calling."

What biblical evidence is there for describing work as mission? The following chapter will provide more details, but passages that describe the overarching meaning of living out the Christian faith certainly apply. In John 20:21, for example, Jesus instructed the disciples, "As the Father has sent me, so I send you." Matthew 28:19, often called the Great Commission, also describes the mission of people of faith, and the workplace is not excluded from this mission.

Other passages that deal more pointedly with the mission of people of faith at work include Paul's household instructions to Christian slaves and masters about how they lived out their faith in their work (see Eph 6:5-9; Col 3:22–4:1). Still another passage that treats this subject is Paul's instruction to the "believers who are living in idleness" at Thessalonica (2 Thess 3:6-12). Their mission? In plain language, get to work!

Sorting Out the Views

Each of the biblical views just summarized has some measure of relevance in providing help in relating faith to daily work and seeing how faith can express itself in work. Only the view of work as curse has no foundation. Each of the other views—work as divine assignment; as an ordinary, expected part of life; as worthy of God's praise and blessing; as an area of God's concern; as calling and vocation; and as mission—can provide assistance in relating faith to daily work.

Work as mission comes closest to providing a summary category, a way of understanding the relation of faith and work. Seeing work as mission leads us to recognize that our work is an integral part of our lives as people of faith. Our work is an expression of our calling to be people of faith, but our calling is larger than our work.

Work as mission can include the idea of work as divine assignment, for included in our mission is the idea of fulfilling a divine assignment. Work as mission also can include the idea of work as an ordinary, expected part of life. Even when one is fulfilling a heavenly purpose, the ordinary affairs of life often are the means one must use to achieve such a purpose. Even people bent on a heavenly mission need eventually to stop and eat. In addition, work as mission can include the idea of work as being worthy of God's praise and blessing. Surely God is pleased with people who follow a mission that is in accord with God's desires.

Furthermore, work as mission can include the idea of work as an area of God's concern, for God is indeed concerned about the conditions in which people express their mission. The idea of work being limited in favor of other purposes also fits with the understanding of work as mission, for work is not the only mission a person likely has. Relating in a healthy manner to one's family might be another mission, for example. Exercising Christian citizenship would be another. The mission at one's job is important, but not all-important.

So, are you called to serve God in your particular job? Simply put, the idea is right, but the word is not the best. What's a better word? It's *mission.* Try thinking of your work as a mission. See how that enables you to relate your work to your faith more effectively.

Notes

[1]Gerhard von Rad, *Genesis: A Commentary,* trans. John H. Marks, The Old Testament Library (Philadelphia: Westminster Press, 1961) 92.

[2]C. U. Wolf, "Labor," *The Interpreter's Dictionary of the Bible* (New York: Abingdon Press, 1962) 3:52.

[3]Dorothee Soelle, with Shirley A. Cloyes, *To Work and to Love* (Philadelphia: Fortress Press, 1984) 90.

[4]Even the attempt to equate Sunday with the Sabbath is suspect, of course.

[5]Robert Wuthnow, *God and Mammon in America* (New York: Free Press, 1994) 69.

[6]Robert N. Bellah et al., *Habits of the Heart: Individualism and Commitment in American Life* (Berkeley CA: University of California Press, 1985) 66.

[7]Ibid.

[8]Ibid., 71.

[9]Robert L. Calhoun, "Work and Vocation in Christian History," *Work and Vocation: A Christian Discussion,* edited and with an introduction by John Oliver Nelson (New York: Harper & Brothers, 1954) 106.

[10]See Mark 1:20. In Romans 1:1, Paul uses another form of the word to describe himself as "called an apostle" or "a called apostle."

[11]"kaleo," *The Theological Dictionary of the New Testament,* Geoffrey W. Bromiley, trans. and ed., Gerhard Kittel, ed., (Grand Rapids MI: Eerdmans, 1965) 3:489.

[12]"klasis," *The Theological Dictionary of the New Testament,* Geoffrey W. Bromiley, trans. and ed., Gerhard Kittel, ed. (Grand Rapids MI: Eerdmans, 1965) 3:491-92n.

[13]"klasis," *A Greek-English Lexicon of the New Testament and Other Early Christian Literature,* William F. Arndt and F. Wilbur Gingrich, eds. (Chicago: University of Chicago Press, 1957) 436.

[14]Alan Richardson, *The Biblical Doctrine of Work* (London: SCM Press Ltd., 1963) 33.

[15]Paul S. Minear, "Work and Vocation in Scripture," *Work and Vocation: A Christian Discussion,* 74.

[16]James W. Fowler, *Becoming Adult, Becoming Christian: Adult Development and Christian Faith* (San Francisco: Harper & Row, 1984) 95.

[17]Miroslav Volf, *Work in the Spirit: Toward a Theology of Work* (New York: Oxford University Press, 1991) vii.

Chapter 3
Can Faith Really Be Lived at Work?

"I look for ways to live my faith at work," said a young woman who worked in the human resources department of a large company. She was attending a seminar I was leading. She went on to mention briefly how she attempted to relate in a humane manner to the employees with whom she came into contact, including people with whom she might be involved in a disciplinary procedure. I was impressed that she seemed to see her work in the secular world as a Christian ministry. I believe she would answer yes to the question, "Can faith really can be lived at work?"

A business leader with more than a few gray hairs and the wisdom and spiritual sensitivity to match them told how he sought to live his faith in the high-level business and governmental work in which he was involved. Indeed, he said, the real test of a church's ministry is how well that church equips its members to live their faith in the world of work. Furthermore, he continued, the real test of a Christian's ministry is how well he or she ministers in the world of work, not simply the number of church activities attended or committees served on. I believe he, too, would answer yes to the question, "Can faith really be lived at work?"

Many people of faith, however, often seem to feel that faith not only *is not* being lived at work but that it *cannot,* mainly because the world of faith and the world of work are so entirely different. These feelings need to be taken seriously, of course. Still, I contend that the best answer to the question, "Can faith really be lived at work?" is yes, not no, and I invite you to consider some reasons for this positive answer. These reasons seem grounded well in biblical teachings, theological reflection, and the experience of Christians through the centuries.

God Loves the World—of Work, Too

Perhaps the most familiar verse in all the Bible to Christians reads like this: "For God so loved the world that he gave his only Son, so that everyone who believes in him may not perish but may have eternal life" (John 3:16). Note: the object of God's love is "the world."

So often our view of "the world" overlooks this assertion from the Gospel of John that God loves *the world*. This world in which you and

I live, God loves. God loves this world, warts and all. This world God loves is the world of people.

Plenty of texts in the New Testament speak of the world as opposed to God. The word "world" is indeed used in the New Testament to depict the opposition of human culture to God. Thus, the Letter of James issues the command that we are to keep ourselves "unstained by the world" (1:27). Too, Paul contrasts "the spirit of the world" to "the Spirit that is from God" (1 Cor 2:12). And 1 John states, "The whole world lies under the power of the evil one" (5:19).

But do such warnings concern the wrong aspects of the world or the world in general? This is the $64 billion question. It has concerned people of faith throughout Christian history. Entire approaches to faith have been founded on the various answers. Through the centuries, Christians have given several basic answers to the question of how people of faith are to view and be related to the world.[1]

Faith is good; the world is bad.

Some people of faith see complete opposition between faith and the world of human culture. They and the churches of which they are a part call for complete separation from that world. At the extreme among such folk would be the radical sects that withdraw from the world and gather on some mountain or in some compound to await the end of the world. Of course, there's a pretty deep strain of this kind of thinking in American Protestantism in general, especially in the conservative and fundamentalist churches.

The history of this view is lengthy. Tertullian, a church leader during the early years of the third century, advised believers

> to withdraw from many meetings and many occupations, not only because they are corrupted by their relation to pagan faith but because they require a mode of life contrary to the spirit and the law of Christ.[2]

You might be surprised to learn which occupations he advised people of faith not to get involved in—or maybe you wouldn't. Among the occupations he counseled against were politics, military service, philosophy, and the arts. He even warned against a career in business. Tertullian said that business "is scarcely 'adapted for a servant of God,' for apart from covetousness, which is a species of idolatry, there is no real motive for acquiring."[3]

What does such a view mean when applied to the world of work? It means that the world of work is always in opposition to the world of faith. In this view, people of faith venture forth from secluded enclaves to carefully selected locations in which they guard themselves vigilantly from the flesh and the devil in the world of work. At the end of the day, or at least on Sunday, they then retreat to the world of faith and take refuge there as soon as they can.

One person said that when she drove by her church as she went about her work, she often felt an overwhelming desire to run in and seek sanctuary from the work of selling in which she was involved in the world. Tertullian and others who hold this view might well say, "Then stop your car, get out of it, run to the church building, and leave the world behind!"

Lots of luck on leaving the world behind, though. One problem with attempting to separate ourselves completely from the world in the manner in which this view suggests is that the world is not just "out there." The world this view attempts to avoid, the world that is unresponsive to God and opposed to God, is already "in us" before we ever venture "out there."

Too, how will the world know that God loves it if people of faith retreat from it and avoid it like the plague? After all, in Jesus' prayer recorded in John 17, he prayed, "As you have sent me into the world, so I have sent them into the world" (v. 18). Earlier, Jesus affirmed to his disciples, "In the world you face persecution." He continued, though, "But take courage; I have conquered the world!" (16:33).

Faith and the world—they look alike to me.

When some people of faith take a look at the world and at faith, everything looks just rosy to them. This view stands at the opposite end of the spectrum from the first view. In the first view, faith rejects everything else as bad; in this view, faith accepts everything else as good. Theologian H. Richard Niebuhr suggested that among those who give this answer,

> Jesus often appears a great hero of human culture history; his life and teachings are regarded as the greatest human achievement; in him, it is believed, the aspirations of men toward their values are brought to a point of culmination; he confirms what is best in the past, and guides the process of civilization to its proper goal.[4]

According to this view, faith and the world are already so intertwined that there is little difference between them. Whenever human culture moves in a direction people perceive to be forward, this view sees Christ as in a sense putting his stamp of approval on it, no questions asked. Logic would suggest that such a view extends to the world of work as well.

In this view, faith becomes *of* the world as well as *in* it. This sort of faith is a sort of lowest-common-denominator approach that pretty much accepts whatever looks like a good thing. After all, why rock the boat by being too serious, and aren't we going to the same place anyway? The shortcoming of this open-minded approach is that it's easy for folks who hold this view to go along with whatever the culture says is good at a given point in time. Not much critical thinking and evaluation occurs, and the claims of faith often get lost.

Some things in the world are good; some aren't.

The third major position people of faith have held about the world is that some things in it are good, and some aren't. One variation on this theme sees people of faith living in the midst of a tension between Christ and the world of human culture. They are torn between obeying one authority or the other.

Niebuhr refers to this variation as the amphibian position, where the ideas and methods of one realm are not used in the other.[5] A great many people of faith attempt to live in such a manner. They try to live in both the world of faith and the world of human culture, but without bringing them together. Like landlubbers, they use their lungs on Sunday. Like sea-dwellers, they use their gills on Monday through Friday. They attempt to be at home in both worlds. But, of course, people of faith aren't amphibians, and so they find themselves gasping for oxygen in the environment in which they live from Monday through Friday. You can hold your breath only so long, you know.

In some respects, this view epitomizes the current approach to work held by many Christians and churches. People of faith find themselves living in two very different ways, all according to the world in which they find themselves at a given moment. Is this Monday, and am I at work? Then these rules apply. Is this Sunday, and is this the world of faith? Then these rules apply.

A better variation on this theme sees the need to find ways to bring the resources of faith into operation in the world itself. What needs to be done is to identify the things that are good and that aren't, be glad about the good, and attempt to transform the not-so-good. In one way or another, to one degree or another, this view pictures Christians being *in* the world, using the good things, but not being so much *of* the world that they cannot see what needs to be improved and become involved in making the needed changes.

How does this view apply to people of faith seeking to live their faith in the world of work? This view suggests that through God's help, people of faith may be able to transform the difficult conditions they face in the world of work and change for the better the things that aren't right. With God's help, the world of work, or at least aspects of it, can be moved from opposition to Christ to service on his behalf.

In his letter to the Philippians, Paul used metaphorical language that suggested the church was to function as a colony of heaven (1:27; 3:20). The manner in which Christians were to conduct their lives was to reflect Christians' position as residing in the world as colonists who have their true citizenship in heaven (3:20). As with other colonists, their goal was—and is—to claim and transform the world for their home country.

Historically, colonists' only reason for being in the strange land was to establish a colony, an outpost, of their home country and thus to claim and transform the land for their home country. Their goal was not to get out of that new land as quickly as possible but to move ever more deeply into the new land and extend the influence of their home country.

The unfortunate history of colonialism should not obscure the meaning of the metaphor or its application to the world of work. Christians in the world of work may find themselves in a position similar to that of the Philippian Christians. They function in a sense as a colony of heaven, an outpost meant to extend the rule of heaven into the world—in this case the world of work—and to transform that world.

So, can faith be lived at work? Yes, because God loves the world—including the world of work.

People of Faith Are Sent into the World to Minister

A second reason for answering yes is that people of faith are sent into the world to serve. Let's examine this reason by looking at three elements summarized in the answer.

People of Faith

Notice that people of faith, not just the people of faith often called "clergy," are sent into the world. In the New Testament, separation between clergy and laity does not exist. Indeed, all Christians are clergy in the New Testament.[6] The meaning of this statement is that all people of faith—laypeople included—are ministers. All people of faith are charged with the task of Christian service.

Those church leaders who might be called "clergy" are people of faith set apart within, not apart from or above, the *laos*. *Laos* is the Greek word that when applied to Christians simply means "the people of God." Unfortunately, through centuries of church history, this perfectly good word, *laos,* was perverted to mean "layperson," someone not trained or qualified for real work. Test the validity of this idea by asking yourself whether you would prefer for a "surgeon" or a "lay surgeon" to perform your next operation!

As Loren Mead, an Episcopal priest and founder of the Alban Institute, says, "Clericalism—like sin—is a good thing taken too far"![7] The "clergy," part of the people of God and set apart within the people of God, are charged with equipping, leading, assisting, and encouraging the rest of the people of God in performing their ministry (Eph 4:11-12). They don't minister *in place of* the people of God but *with* them.

A biblical interpreter of an earlier day, T. W. Manson, wrote these lines that serve to focus the importance of these thoughts for both Christian history and today:

> The Christianity that conquered the Roman Empire was not an affair of brilliant preachers addressing packed congregations. . . . The great preachers came after Constantine the Great; and before that Christianity had already done its work and made its way right through the Empire from end to end. When we try to picture how it was done we seem to see domestic servants teaching Christ in and through their domestic service, workers doing it through their work, small shopkeepers through their trade, and so on, rather than eloquent propagandists swaying mass meetings of interested inquirers.[8]

That is the way Christian service gets done today, too. It gets done mostly by the people often called "laypeople" or "laity." Indeed, at least 99 percent of it *must* get done by laypeople if it gets done.

Why this bold statement about the crucial nature of the ministry of laypeople? Their sheer numbers in comparison to clergy, for one thing, support this statement. In addition, clergy do not—and, indeed, are unable to—go into all of the places where Christian ministry needs to be done. Furthermore, a crucial place where laypeople go and clergy cannot or do not go is the workplace.

Sent into the World

The model for Christian service is not the prophet Elijah, moping about in a deserted cave, far from the centers of power, bemoaning his fate (1 Kgs 19:4-18). Indeed, this experience was not characteristic of Elijah himself. He ordinarily was actively engaged in the public life of his day, too actively for the rulers and religious leaders whose views and actions he opposed.

Even so, the supreme model for Christian service is of course Jesus, whom God sent into the world. Christians refer to this event as the incarnation. The incarnation literally means "enfleshment" and refers to God's "enfleshment" of His son. The incarnation was God's sending of His son into the *world.*

Moreover, John 20:21 spells out plainly that Christians are sent as Jesus was sent. Jesus said to his disciples, "As the Father has sent me, so I send you." The ministry of the disciples was to continue the ministry of Christ himself. The good news of Jesus is to be incarnated —enfleshed—in his people.

T. W. Manson was right on target again when he wrote, "There is only one 'essential ministry' in the church, the perpetual ministry of the risen and ever-present Lord himself."[9] And people of faith continue that ministry because he has sent us to perform it.

A further part of the "as" of John 20:21 is the idea that we are to continue to seek to accomplish the task of Christ's ministry in the setting in which he ministered. What is the setting? The world.

We noted earlier John 17:15, which records Jesus praying for his disciples, including us, with these words, "I am not asking you to take them out of the world, but I ask you to protect them from the evil one." In verse 18, he continues to be explicit, praying, "As you have sent me into the world, so I have sent them into the world."

So Jesus sends his disciples into the world. What is the task? One way of expressing it is in John 10:10, where Jesus says, "I came that they may have life, and have it abundantly." Because that was his task, that is also the task of Jesus' disciples as they continue Jesus' ministry in the world, including the world of work. The task is to enable people to experience life and to experience it abundantly.

Would this be a tall order in the place where you work? Most likely. But its difficulty does not remove the challenge that it is the task of people of faith.

Dag Hammarskjold was Secretary-General of the United Nations in the 1950s. His book *Markings,* published after his death in an airplane crash while on United Nations business, revealed that he was also a deeply spiritual person. These words from the book are relevant to Christians as they seek to continue Christ's ministry in the world. They apply especially to the world of work. "In our era," he wrote, "the road to holiness necessarily passes through the world of action."[10] The world of work fits in that world of action, where people of faith are sent.

To Minister

Look more closely at the purpose for which people of faith are sent into the world. Simply put, if they continue Christ's ministry, then it is inescapable that they are sent to serve, to minister.

Mark 10:45 is what may be called a climactic text, a verse that captures great truths in a few words. There Jesus said of himself that "the Son of Man came not be served but to serve, and to give his life a ransom for many."

Jesus personalized this truth throughout his ministry. He made it extremely personal, too personal in fact, for his disciples in the incident recounted in John 13. The setting of this passage is Jesus' last supper before his crucifixion. The passage describes how he

> got up from the table, took off his outer robe, and tied a towel around himself. Then he poured water into a basin and began to wash the disciples' feet and to wipe them with the towel that was tied around him. (vv. 4-5)

He then audaciously told the astonished, humbled disciples, "I have set you an example, that you also should do as I have done to you" (v. 15).

Longtime professor of New Testament Frank Stagg observed, "The greatest title which one may receive is not 'Master' or 'Father' or 'Teacher'; it is 'Servant' " (cf. Matt 23:6-11).[11] How does this thought apply to the world of work? Radically.

Is the greatest title in the world of work boss, manager, vice-president, or president? Or is it servant? Listen to these words from magazine publishing executive James Autry:

> Good management is largely a matter of love. Or if you're uncomfortable with that word, call it caring, because proper management involves caring for people, not manipulating them.[12]

He even dares to say, "If you don't care about people, get out of management before it's too late."[13] When you talk about caring about people, being a servant to them cannot be far behind, whatever your title at work.

Jan Carlzon, chief executive of Scandinavian Airlines System, spoke even more pointedly when he told his managers that they were not to feel superior to or more important than the front-line workers.

"When they come to you with problems, you have to listen to them and help them, not the other way around," he said.[14]

But would being a servant really work at work? The answer is yes. As the customer service emphasis in business continues to grow, and as management grows in its perception that treating customers right calls first for treating employees right, with any luck we may see a humanizing of business—which may include an acceptance of the servant role. Indeed, the businesses that succeed for the long term do live by the servant role. In such businesses, this attitude and practice is part of the culture that guides the relationships of employees with employees, employees with management, and everyone with customers.

Unfortunately, business does not recognize universally the importance of this concept. Because it doesn't, it's important to ask what could happen if people of faith put it into practice in a work setting that failed to recognize its value. Would they run aground on the prevailing management system? Would they make less money? Would they fail to get promoted? Would someone think their actions laughable—and actually laugh at them? If, however, in the real world of business, actions of service such as caring and integrity are not necessarily rewarded, this doesn't mean people of faith shouldn't do them, does it?

The humorous movie *Oh, God* from a few years back carried a serious message at points. Toward the end of the movie, God, played by entertainer George Burns, is advising the young man who had attempted to deliver God's message to a world that did not want to hear it. The young man had lost his job and was disconsolate. God says words to this effect, "Well, lose a job, save a world—not a bad deal." Sounds heretical and radical, doesn't it?

Now consider a third answer to the question, "Can faith really be lived at work?"

The World of Work Is an
Arena for the Use of One's Gifts

The New Testament teaches that all Christians have been given gifts to be used in Christian service. The most extensive treatment of this teaching is in 1 Corinthians 12, especially verses 4-10 and 28-30. Other references are Romans 12:6-8; Ephesians 4:11; and 1 Peter 4:10-11.

If you took time to compare the gifts mentioned in each of these passages, you would find that the gifts named in the references vary. This variation in the lists supports the idea that the intention of these passages is not to name all of the gifts given to people of faith. It's reasonable to assume that other gifts exist.

In spite of the variation in the lists of gifts in the New Testament references, there are at least two constants in the teaching about gifts being given to people of faith. One constant is who gives the gifts— God. A second constant is the purpose of the gifts—the common good (1 Cor 12:7).

Readers and interpreters of these passages have often assumed that these gifts are to be used only within the church and sometimes only on church property. This assumption ignores two factors. First, the work of the church—God's people, people of faith—is in the world, not simply in public worship and religious ritual. Second, the church existed and did well for several hundred years, thank you, without owning property. Would it not be more true to God's intent for people of faith to consider the gifts God gives as being usable and, indeed, intended for use wherever they are, including at work?

The world of work needs the good that can come when people of faith employ in the work setting the gifts God has given them. The world of work needs people of faith to use the gifts of leadership, administration, faithfulness, encouragement, sensitivity, caring, and clear communication—just to name a few. It needs the gifts embedded in the ability to compute long, complicated sets of figures, to figure out how to build things, to repair things, and to do all of the other kinds of tasks needed in our society.

In the country community where I once served as pastor, the gifts of many people were required to make life work. The interrelated nature of church and work, church and community, resulted in there being no clear line between gifts used "within the church" and "at work" and "in the community."

The person, for example, who had what I want to suggest was the gift of plumbing, found himself being a plumber in his full-time work for the school, in his assistance in keeping the church's buildings in good repair, and in his help to many people in the community. I'm fully convinced that plumbing in his case was a Christian gift and Shelton used it as such, regardless of the setting in which he found himself. Furthermore, as one who knows what it's like not to have indoor plumbing, I believe I am on solid theological ground in calling plumbing a gift! If you've lived all your life with indoor plumbing, let me tell you forthrightly that you are in absolutely no position to question whether plumbing is a gift, no matter how many theological degrees you may have. Thank you, Shelton, for your use of your gift.

I believe that God intends us to use our gifts in whatever setting service is needed. Where does the Bible say that God's gifts are to be used only in the church house or at church gatherings? Rather, the use of gifts is not limited to church gatherings, church ritual, or church property. The use of gifts, therefore, extends to our participation in the world of work. As Thomas Merton, the businessman who became a Catholic monk, wrote:

> The work of each Christian must be not only honest and decent, it must not only be productive, but it should contribute a positive service to human society. It should have a part in the general striving of all men for a peaceful and well-ordered civilization in this world, for in that way it best helps us to prepare for the next world.[15]

Because of the gifts God has given us, through every part of our lives—including our work—we can accomplish such goals.

Faith Can Be Lived at Work

So, *can* faith really be lived at work? My conclusion is absolutely yes. Indeed, it must. Of course, in answering yes, we cannot and must not deny that it's easier to see some jobs better than others as being opportunities for Christian service. In fact, probably most people of faith feel the difficulty some of the time about even the jobs with the greatest potential of being perceived as avenues of Christian service.

Sugarcoating the difficulties of living faith at work is neither wise nor helpful. Some jobs are filled with only the emptiness of dull routine. As Rosemary Barciauskas and Debra Hull suggest:

> When I put the same small part into an electronics board hour after hour, or when I must clean offices at night for people I never see, it is difficult to think of one's labor as a vocation, or even as part of God's call to me. . . . When there is no possibility of a creative contribution of my uniqueness to a job, when there is no opportunity to feel its connectedness to an overall project that is worth doing, or to the community it serves, it is difficult and perhaps even harmful to conceive our labor as part of God's call to us.[16]

The truth that the situation at our jobs may make living our faith in the world of work difficult does not free us from the obligation to seek ways to do so, however. The ideas of this chapter are meant to emphasize that faith both *can* be lived at work and that it is *intended* to be lived there.

I was struck by a statement near the beginning of Robert Redford's movie, *A River Runs Through It.* The narrator is describing his boyhood in Montana. He was one of two sons of a Presbyterian minister who loved to fly-fish and taught his sons to love it, too. The narrator said that in his family there was "no clear line between religion and fly-fishing."

That's the way it should be with work, too. There should be no clear line between religion and daily work. Perhaps the ideal is that work itself become a truly religious experience. Faith really can be lived at work, and it must.

Notes

[1]Theologian H. Richard Niebuhr gathered and summarized five basic answers in his classic book, *Christ and Culture* (New York: Harper & Row, 1951) 40-43.

[2]Tertullian, *On Idolatry,* xi, quoted in Niebuhr, 53-54.

[3]Ibid., 54.

[4]Niebuhr, 41.

[5]Ibid., 183.

[6]Philip Schaff, *History of the Christian Church* (New York: Charles Scribner's Sons, 1911) 2:124.

[7]Loren B. Mead, *The Once and Future Church: Reinventing the Congregation for a New Mission Frontier* (Washington DC: The Alban Institute, 1991) 33.

[8]T. W. Manson, *Ministry and Priesthood* (Richmond VA: John Knox Press, n.d.) 21.

[9]T. W. Manson, *The Church's Ministry* (Philadelphia: Westminster Press, 1948) 107.

[10]Dag Hammarskjold, *Markings,* trans. from the Swedish by Leif Sjoberg and W. H. Auden, with a foreword by W. H. Auden (New York: Alfred A. Knopf, 1969) 122.

[11]Frank Stagg, *New Testament Theology* (Nashville TN: Broadman Press, 1962) 253.

[13]James Autry, *Love and Profit* (New York: William Morrow & Co., Inc.) 13.

[12]Ibid, 17, italics in the original.

[14]Jan Carlzon, quoted in Karl Albrecht, *Service Within: Solving the Middle Management Leadership Crisis* (Homewood Il: Business One Irwin, 1990) 4.

[15]Thomas Merton, *Life and Holiness* (New York: Doubleday, 1963) 9-10.

[16]Rosemary Curren Barciauskas and Debra Beery Hull, *Loving and Working: Reweaving Women's Public and Private Lives* (Bloomington IN: Meyer-Stone Books, 1989) 122.

Chapter 4
Find and Follow Your Personal Purpose in Life

A friend's grandparents lived and worked in Arizona during the early decades of the 1900s, just as Arizona was achieving statehood. They chose and followed a pattern for their lives that many would consider unusual. They would move to a small town and set up their business. Along with their business, however, they would establish a church and nurture it until its resources were sufficient to support a pastor of its own. The couple then would move to the next town and start the process all over again. A purpose, a mission, dominated their lives, and it included how they approached their daily work.

A purpose dominates your life and your approach to your daily work, too. That purpose determines what you value, how you act, how you relate to coworkers, and any number of other attitudes and actions. How clear is that purpose to you? How consciously have you chosen it? Is it as satisfying and all-encompassing as you would like it to be?

Many people, including people of faith, merely drift into their purpose for living or settle too soon for a purpose that is fragmented, incomplete, or otherwise fails to be worthy of their best efforts. They do this rather than choosing consciously a focused, comprehensive, fulfilling purpose for their lives, including their lives at work. Such failure to choose and focus one's purpose causes much of the frustration and dissatisfaction with their work lives that many people feel.

Recognize the Importance of the Right Purpose

A cartoon portrays two weary mountain climbers reaching the peak of their mountain. Their brief sense of elation turns quickly to disappointment as they look around them, though. They become distressed when they see on all sides of them peaks significantly higher and thus more inviting than the one they had labored so hard to climb.

Choosing the right mountain comes high on the list of things to do to get ready for mountain-climbing. Similarly, choosing the right purpose comes at the top of the list of things to do in living faith in daily work. Why is choosing the right purpose so important? If we are not climbing the right mountain, then every step, whether hard-earned or easy, just takes us farther away from our destiny, not toward it. In the same way, if we have not identified the right purpose for our lives and sought to follow it, every action at work will take us further away from that purpose.

It's hard to pick up any business magazine or business book these days and not find the words "total quality management" or the acronym TQM somewhere in it. Total quality management refers to the practice of business management that looks for better ways of doing things at work so as to maximize productivity. Rightly used, total quality management produces excellent results for all concerned —employees, employers, and customers. Really, total quality management is just the practice of good management.

Any TQM effort begins here: Determine the mission or purpose of the organization. All the rest of the principles of total quality management have to do with aligning the processes and personnel of the business with that mission or purpose. Having the right purpose is the starting point. This is the case with our personal and work lives, too. The starting point is choosing and following the right purpose.

Such a conscious commitment to the right purpose, a truly fulfilling purpose, serves us well when we make the easy choices in our work life; it's indispensable when we must make the hard choices that often come. To avoid drifting through our work life or succumbing to temptations to be less than our best, we need a clear sense of what is truly sacred to us. Knowing what is most valuable to us will help us to understand better when to risk the less valuable, including our jobs themselves, in order to hold on to the things most dear.

Moreover, without a settled sense of purpose, we are adrift, with no firm direction for life sufficient to enable us to deal effectively with the inevitable changes and challenges that occur at work. We need a settled conviction about who we are, what we value, and what our goals are. Choosing the right purpose deserves careful attention.

Be Honest About Your Current Purpose

What is important to you? No matter what a person may say, the answer to this question can be seen in such matters as these: How do you use your time? How do you choose to use your money? How do you relate to people? What unforeseen events—interruptions—upset you or bring you joy? Think about it. If you took some time to evaluate your life by such measures, what would they reveal about what your genuine purposes in living are?

One corporation for which I worked had a wellness program that called for an annual personal evaluation of my health habits. Before I went for my wellness check, I was asked to describe my dietary practices—what vegetables, fruit, dessert, and other food I ate, how often, and how much. Recalling such things was revealing, of course.

One year, though, instead of just recalling what I had eaten, I kept a log, tracking what I ate for a week or so. Now that was revealing! What I actually ate and what I chose to recall having eaten were somehow a bit different. I don't know how that happened.

You would benefit by keeping a log for a representative week or month of your life to identify how you really spend your time and money and how you really relate to people, at work as well as beyond work. Keeping such a log would help you identify the purpose you really follow. For example, if you actually value personal growth, whether on the job or in your personal life, you'll be spending time and money to achieve that growth. Too, if you value people, there will be evidences of that value in your calendar and your checkbook. If you ever keep such a record, be sure to track what irritates you, too, for the irritants reveal the opposites of what you value.

Try a mental exercise that may aid you in determining your purpose and whether you are satisfied with it. Imagine that today is a very special day in your life. It's your 100th birthday. Congratulations! You look marvelous. Willard from the "Today" show has just called your name on national television and wished you a happy birthday. A reporter from the local television station is present, in fact, and by your side, microphone in hand. Your living room is filled with television cameras, friends, family, and a few people whose faces you remember but whose names escape you at the moment.

The reporter is there to interview you and give you the opportunity to tell a bit about your life. She wishes you a happy birthday, too, and asks you to look back on your life. She then asks you these questions:

- What would you say are the four most important things you have done in your life?
- How did you accomplish them?
- What advice would you give to others about what's important in life and how to live it?

You clear your throat, smile at the camera, and anser. What do you say? Your answers to these questions may offer clues about what you really would like your purpose in life to be, whatever it is now. These answers may also encourage you to ask yourself what you're doing now to accomplish that purpose.

State the Purpose Toward
Which You Want to Live Your Life

Let me tell you about a young man whose story seems almost unbe-lievable. His name was Joe—Joe Jacobson. He was an interesting fellow. He was the kind of fellow people loved or hated, with few people being lukewarm about him.

Joe Jacobson was the youngest son in a large family, but he was his father's favorite boy. He had a bright future ahead of him, for he was destined to run the family business. That didn't go over well with his older brothers; they became exceedingly jealous of him. They looked for and found a way to get him in trouble and, unbelievably, to get him trapped into leaving home.

Joe's troubles didn't end when he left home. He found himself far, far away from home, where he didn't know a soul. Joe, though, had such great talents that he soon found himself in a good job as the right-hand man of a very important person. His boss appreciated him, but the boss's wife appreciated Joe even more. She tried to lure Joe into committing adultery with her. Joe remembered his religious values, however, and refused to participate in what he considered to be a sin. At this, the woman accused Joe of attempted rape and had him put into prison. Does this story sound like the latest thriller from Hollywood?

Of course, by now you may have recognized this story as the story of Joseph in the Bible (see Gen 37, 39). The rest of the story pictures Joseph as the second-most important person in all of Egypt, assisting Pharaoh in preserving the nation from famine.

When Joseph's brothers came to buy food in order to save their family back in the land of Palestine from dying of starvation, Joseph recognized them. He did not take vengeance on them, however. Instead, he instituted a test to determine whether the brothers had any sorrow over how they had mistreated him.

At long last, Joseph revealed himself to his brothers. He explained his purpose in life like this: "God sent me before you to preserve life. . . . God sent me before you to preserve for you a remnant on earth, and to keep alive for you many survivors. So it was not you who sent me here, but God; he has made me a father to Pharaoh, and lord of all his house and ruler over all the land of Egypt" (Gen 45:5b, 7-8). Even with all the twists and turns of his life, Joseph understood his spiritual purpose for living to be fulfilled in this very practical work by which he preserved his own people from starvation. He likely could not have fulfilled that purpose if he had not been clear about and faithful to his religious beliefs and values in times of temptation and challenge.

What is your purpose in living? Is it clear enough to sustain you in times of challenge and difficulty? Is it big enough, comprehensive enough, to truly guide your life? If you accomplish that purpose, will you feel that you have lived the most fulfilling life possible? No? Then, it's time to choose another purpose.

Have you taken the time and made the effort to think about, say to yourself, and, even better, write down what your purpose in life is? If so, you're far ahead of most people. All too few have accomplished this all-important task. You need to give some thought to this, though, if you're serious about improving the way you live your faith at work.

E. F. Schumacher put his own purpose in life this way in his book *Good Work:*

> My only business, the only real job we have, is to look after, to the best of our ability, the little people who can't help themselves. If education and the advantages that we have had from society are only so that we might form a sort of trade union of the privileged, then our soul is so burdened with darkness that life is not worth living.[1]

Schumacher felt strongly enough about this purpose that he spent his life seeking ways to improve the work environment of people all over the world by making work more humane.

Millard Fuller is the president and founder of Habitat for Humanity, which builds and renovates houses so that poor people will have decent houses in which to live and grow into all that God intended. He once pursued wealth with all his might and was successful in his efforts. When he became worth $1 million, he announced that his goal was $10 million. When he was confronted by how much he lacked in life and how far he had strayed from God, he gave all the money away. He and his wife now devote themselves to doing God's work through Habitat for Humanity.[2]

What do you feel strongly enough about that it truly has become your purpose for living? Have you stated that purpose in terms practical enough to live out day by day? If not, likely your purpose is so hazy it's of little use in the day-to-day grind of life, especially your work life. Or your purpose may be, as someone suggested about a person who was religious in the worst way, so heavenly-minded that it's of no earthly good.

In his perennial bestselling book on careers, *What Color Is Your Parachute?* Richard Bolles gives guidance for finding one's personal mission in life. He suggests that one's mission or purpose can best be summarized in three major points: (1) to seek to live in constant communion with God, (2) to follow God's leading in seeking to make a positive difference in the world, and (3) to do so by exercising our unique talent, the one we most like to use, in the place we like the best, and for the work God most needs to have done.[3] Bolles maintains that the career one chooses should contribute to, not detract from, such purposes for living.

At the risk of sounding more pious than I want to appear or actually may be, let me tell you how I arrived at my sense of purpose in life. When I was a teenager graduating from high school, I found in the words of Matthew 6:33 an expression of my overall purpose in life. These words of Jesus read as follows: "Seek ye first the kingdom of God, and all these things shall be added unto you."

Of course, these thoughts come from the section in Jesus' Sermon on the Mount where Jesus cautioned against the quest for material things, which do not last, do not provide the highest value to be desired, and thus are not worthy of our deepest devotion. On the other hand, Jesus instructed his followers to seek the kingdom of God, which does indeed last, provide the highest value to be desired, and thus is worthy of our lives. However far short I have come in truly living these words, they have served through the years as a firm touchstone for my life. I've changed my strategy for living several times and may well do so again, but I've tried to keep headed toward the goal set forth in Matthew 6:33.

Matthew 6:33 becomes especially helpful when I recall that the kingdom of God refers to the rule of God and describes a condition in which God's will is done on earth as it is in heaven. The kingdom of God is the time, place, and condition of life in which the justice, love, and grace of God prevail and one's relationship to God is unimpaired.

When I interpret and apply Matthew 6:33 in such a manner, this verse provides the basis for making applications to my everyday life, including my life at work. When I am at my best, I recognize all daily choices that cannot fit with these words to be cheap distractions from my chosen purpose if not fully at odds with it.

The lofty words of Matthew 6:33 need further specification if I am to do much about them, however. So, I've found it helpful to write out my Mission in life. That Mission—capitalized to indicate that it is all-encompassing—includes my mission in my work. I currently state it like this:

> My mission in life is to be a servant of all as a follower of Christ and member of Christ's people, using my unique gifts and opportunities to express this mission in these roles I have chosen to honor: person of faith; family member; writer; seminar leader; consultant; and growing, healthy person involved in positive human relationships.

Included in this statement are references to the various roles in life that are important to me. In each of these roles, I've tried to specify my intentions in these areas and clarify how my actions in these roles reflect my understanding of seeking the kingdom of God. These roles reflect who I understand myself to be as a result of my heredity, the environments in which I have lived and by which I have been influenced, the opportunities that have come my way, and the choices I have made and that yet appear open to me. They're also roles I enjoy. Is God involved in these roles, whether thrust upon me or chosen by me? Absolutely.

How is God involved? Foremost, God offered me the potential of living as a person of faith. The theological word for that act is "grace." God also put me into my family of origin in a particular place and time and enabled me to establish a family of my own. Further, God enabled me to have certain gifts and skills and to enjoy employing them in certain settings at various stages of life. Too, God opens my eyes to needs in which the unique "I" that I am can be put to use in creative, helpful ways in God's world.

I see each of these roles as joyful opportunities for practicing justice, demonstrating love, and extending grace to situations and people who need justice, love, and grace. Frederick Buechner put it most attractively when he wrote, "The place God calls you to is the place where your deep gladness and the world's deep hunger meet."[4]

All must come to their own conclusions about their mission and roles, of course. In fact, I reserve for myself the right to change my definition and expression of my own roles as time moves along. Still, these roles and a more detailed statement of intention for each of them provide a useful way for me to understand and express my own current purpose.

When I was a teenager and then a young adult, I viewed in a rather mystical manner the matter of finding God's will in the various roles of my life. I still have a mystical view of the matter of finding God's will, believing that one way God reveals God's desires for us is through our feelings and intuitions. Still, incorporated into that mystical view is now a belief that God works through quite practical means and seemingly mundane circumstances.

Many people of faith are at once too spiritual and not at all spiritual enough as they consider their careers, their daily work. They are too spiritual in that they fail to take account of the very practical ways in which God moves in our lives—through our genes, our circumstances, and our opportunities. They are not spiritual enough because they fail to realize that the most mundane circumstance is a part of what makes up one's being a spiritual person.

Think about it. Wasn't the most spiritual person who ever lived born as a little baby? Recall what a baby is like. Is anything the source of greater awe than a baby? As a father and a grandfather, my answer is No! But there's more. Does anything or anyone need more intensely practical activity than a little baby? Again I say, No! Mundane matters such as being fed, having a diaper changed, and being held seem to hold vastly more importance to a baby than abstract philosophizing about the meaning of life.

Consider another example. Exodus 3 tells how Moses met God at the burning bush, an intensely spiritual experience. Through that spiritual experience, God confronted Moses with the task God wanted Moses to accomplish. The two earlier chapters of Exodus, however, give insight into how God likely used the experiences of everyday life as a part of Moses' preparation for his future. One significant such factor was that Moses, though a Hebrew, was reared as the son of Pharaoh's daughter and thus would have received the education that others of Pharaoh's household received.

As you consider your own roles and how you can express your purpose in life through them, be both intensely practical and intensely spiritual. Any purpose that does not qualify on both counts is too narrow, too shortsighted, and too limited. A purpose that is not intensely spiritual fails to recognize the dimension of faith. A purpose that is not intensely practical fails to perceive that life must be lived in a very practical world, where competence in a given area stands for more than a vague feeling that one ought to take a certain course of action. If you were facing surgery, for example, wouldn't you want a surgeon who is skilled rather than a person who simply believes he can do it, has prayed about it, but has never demonstrated his skill successfully?

Dave Thomas, founder of Wendy's, states that one reason he went into the restaurant business was because he believed that feeding people was the work God had called him to do. He combined an intensely spiritual purpose with the very practical skills of serving food that lots of people like and marketing it successfully—very successfully.[5]

Do you want to relate your faith more effectively to your work? Then start by taking the time to determine your purpose for living. Identify the all-encompassing roles of your life, and state how you can live out that purpose in each of those roles. Actually write them down so you will look at them and consider them seriously. Include both the practical and the spiritual dimensions of life as you do. Are you satisfied with each of these roles? Do they represent the real you? Or are some of these roles leading you away from the person you wish to be? You may need to modify or even discard such roles.

You would benefit by taking this exercise a step further. Draw a circle large enough to include smaller circles representing the same number of roles you have just identified and listed. Actually draw these circles. Then ask yourself this question: Of the roles you have listed, which role would come closest to representing the unifying role that encompasses all the other roles of your life? Is there one? If not, I suggest you need to find one. For me, the role I've chosen to label "person of faith" would be the large circle. This is the role that gives coherence, integrity, and meaning to all of the other roles of my life.

Perry Bigelow, a person who seeks to live out his faith as a home builder, says it well:

> There are two ways to connect faith and work. One can integrate faith and work, in which case faith is secondary to work, or one can integrate work into faith, in which case faith is primary. I have tried both ways. For me, integrating faith into work resulted in compartmentalization; integrating work into faith is holistic.[6]

I too believe you will find the results the same.

So, make faith the largest circle of your life; fit everything else, including work, in that circle; and discard or transform everything that won't fit. This approach will enable you to sort through the challenges and opportunities that come your way—including those at work—and live with purpose, not aimlessness, and a greater sense of wholeness, not fragmentation. Isn't this what we want?

Make Your Purpose Specific in a Place of Work

The first point at which our life purpose should enter our work life is in our choice of a job. It's important that we examine any job we're considering for its alignment with our purpose. As Thomas Moore, psychotherapist, former Catholic monk, and bestselling author, suggests:

> If a potential employer describes all the benefits of a job, we could ask about the soul values. What is the spirit in this workplace? Will I be treated as a person here? Is there a feeling of community? Do people love their work? Is what we are doing and producing worthy of my commitment and long hours? Are there any moral problems in the job or workplace—making things detrimental to people or to the earth, taking excessive profits or contributing to racial and sexist oppression?[7]

These questions represent spiritual matters, of course, but they have very practical, day-to-day applications to life at work. Life is too short not to consider such questions as you choose a job. Why bother to spend your days building a house on sand, a structure that will not last? Why not choose to find a job that is more in harmony with your own sense of purpose? Making a living is important, but why not choose a job that enables you to make a difference as well as make a living?

But what if I'm already in a job, you may ask? Then, if the job otherwise fits with your sense of purpose, you must seek ways day by day to live out that sense of purpose as you fulfill the responsibilities expected of you. This is a second point at which your life purpose should affect your work life.

Most of us find ourselves doing some incredibly mundane work on a rather regular basis—a good bit of every day if not all of the time. I doubt we can see in such work much sense of spiritual purpose. Among the hallmarks of aspects of many jobs, in fact, is their repetitive nature. That, and the sense that doing them has little or no eternal significance. At least if such eternal significance exists, it's disguised very cleverly behind a this-worldly exterior.

To insist that we recognize an eternal purpose for each task would be both naive and impossible, however. Such an insistence would also fail to recognize that high purposes generally have to be achieved through just such mundane acts. What kind of workplace would we have if the garbage didn't get taken out, the toner didn't get changed in the copier, or the electricity stopped working? It would be a workplace that soon would not function.

A veteran mail deliverer in an office was orienting the new employee who would replace him. "Remember," he said, "you have the most important job in this building. If these people don't get their mail, they can't do their work of producing publications that will help people." I think he saw a definite high purpose in what seemed to be a mundane act.

Near the end of the nineteenth century, a young minister in Kansas became concerned about the conditions that existed in the city in which he served and about what he considered to be the lack of Christian response to those conditions. He wrote a novel to present the problem and its solution. Its title, *In His Steps,* is taken from 1 Peter 1:21: "For to this you have been called, because Christ also suffered for you, leaving you an example, so that you should follow in his steps."

In His Steps first appeared in 1897 and portrays what happened when a small group of people began to take their faith seriously. They vowed to ask themselves this question about their actions: What would Jesus do?

One of the characters in the novel was Milton Wright, a business-man. Wright faced the novel's question and developed this list of actions he believed Jesus would take:

1. He would engage in the business first of all for the purpose of glorifying God, and not for the primary purpose of making money.
2. All money that might be made he would never regard as his own, but as trust funds to be used for the good of humanity.
3. His relations with all the persons in his employ would be the most loving and helpful. He could not help thinking of all of them in the light of souls to be saved. This thought would always be greater than his thought of making money in the business.
4. He would never do a single dishonest or questionable thing or try in any remote way to get the advantage of anyone else in the same business.
5. The principle of unselfishness and helpfulness in the business would direct all its details.
6. Upon this principle he would shape the entire plan of his relations to his employees, to the people who were his customers, and to the general business world with which he was connected.[8]

The very words of these statements seem dated and dusty. Even beyond the words, the thoughts themselves seem antiquated, quite unrealistic, and certainly out of place in the modern world of business. Granting all this, however, we would do well to pay attention to the moral and religious commitment behind these statements rather than simply dismiss them as unrealistic and not applicable to our day.

Truth be told, those words were quite out of place in the day in which they were written, for the 1890s were a time of great challenge for business and society, just as today is. A key question of our day, as well as of that day, concerns the manner in which business will be con-ducted and with what effect on the people of the society of which business is a part. Now, as well as then, serious people of faith are being challenged to consider their purpose for living and how it applies to their actions in the world of work. Some people are seeking to do this not just for themselves personally but also to use their influ-ence in their companies to help their companies develop and implement a mission that is meaningful and represents the values they hold dear as individuals. That's the ideal; it's not easy, but it's more than worth a try.[9]

Thomas Merton said, "Christian holiness in our age means more than ever the awareness of our common responsibility to cooperate with the mysterious designs of God for the human race."[10] Finding your purpose and following it in specific ways—including in your work—is crucial to your participation in this cooperative effort.

Notes

[1]Ernst Friedrich Schumacher, *Good Work* (New York: Harper & Row, 1979) 100.

[2]Millard Fuller, *The Theology of the Hammer* (Macon GA: Smyth & Helwys, 1994) 33-37.

[3]Richard Nelson Bolles, *What Color Is Your Parachute? A Practical Manual for Job-Hunters & Career Changers* (Berkeley CA: Ten Speed Press, 1988) 295-96.

[4]Frederick Buechner, *Wishful Thinking: A Theological ABC* (New York: Harper & Row, 1973) 86.

[5]R. David Thomas, "Just Plain Dave," *Higher Than the Top* (Nashville TN: Dimensions for Living, 1993) 88.

[6]Perry Bigelow, "The Builder-Developer as a Steward of God's Resources: Bringing God's Kingdom to the Marketplace and Inner City," *Faith Goes to Work: Reflections from the Marketplace,* Robert J. Banks, comp. (Washington DC: The Alban Institute, 1993) 54.

[7]Thomas Moore, *Care of the Soul: A Guide for Cultivating Depth and Sacredness in Everyday Life* (New York: HarperCollins, 1992) 187.

[8]Charles M. Sheldon, *In His Steps* (Nashville TN: Broadman Press, 1973) 62.

[9]See the story of how Tom Chappell led his company to develop and implement its mission in Tom Chappell, *The Soul of a Business: Managing for Profit and the Common Good* (New York: Bantam, 1993).

[10]Thomas Merton, *Life and Holiness* (New York: Doubleday, 1963) 10.

Chapter 5
Live By Faith's Values

A corporation was planning to survey its customers about their satisfaction with the service they were receiving. The managers responsible believed an anonymous survey was required in order to encourage customers to be completely forthright in their responses. The company still wanted, however, to know what individual customers thought of them. What could they do?

Someone thought of numbering the surveys in a secretive, cryptic manner so the customers who responded to the survey could be identified but would not know it. Pretty clever, huh? The work team responsible for the survey thought so, for that's what they did.

Imagine if you had been involved in the project. Would you have had a problem with what was eventually done? If your answer is yes, what would have been the problem? Would the issue have challenged your sense of right and wrong?

Take the matter a step further. Would you have gone along with sending the survey in the manner described? After all, the goal was good, and what harm could be done if such a mild case of deceit was involved? What if you were the only person on the work team who had a problem with the matter? What if your boss was chairperson of the work team?

I don't know whether anyone on that work team had a problem with sending the survey out in the manner in which they did. The person who reported on what they did certainly did not seem to have a problem with it. Is an ethical issue involved? Is it too small or too subtle to worry with?

Ethical Challenges in the Workplace

People of faith face ethical issues on a regular basis. Some of these issues are bold and obvious, while some are subtle and easily passed over. People of faith are sensitive to the ethical dimensions of some matters they face, but they may so successfully compartmentalize their lives that they fail to see the relevance of faith's values to other work decisions and actions.

Furthermore, it's altogether too easy to believe we are acting according to Christian principles when all we're doing is following the accepted business standards of the business community. James Autry tells how he wants to respond when he hears a businessperson say he runs his business according to Christian principles. Autry says he wants to ask what the businessperson means. Does the person mean, for example, loving his enemies, meaning the competition? Does he mean turning the other cheek when he's been wronged?[1]

In addition, if people of faith work for a corporation, they may retreat behind the notion that corporations are not really subject to the same sorts of ethical standards as individuals. It's possible for people to assume that acts they undertake on behalf of the corporation really don't count when tallying up ethical successes and failures. They may begin to feel that financial profits are all that matter.

Even corporations are not faceless, impersonal entities. They are human institutions, composed of individuals and subject to the same sorts of ethical standards that individual human beings are. This responsibility falls the more heavily on people of faith the more influence they have in and on the corporation.

Even more challenging is the fact that even when we see the ethical dimensions of such work decisions and actions, we may be reluctant to apply our faith to some of these matters because of the cost that might be required. Theologian Matthew Fox, writing on the spiritual dimension of work, makes this challenging statement that people of faith ought to ponder deeply:

> I seriously question the spiritual and ethical life of anyone whose work has never gotten him or her into trouble—if no issues of conscience have ever emerged or no clash of values has been experienced with the ongoing guardians of the status quo. After all, it was Jesus' work that got him into trouble. Christians who claim to follow in his footsteps ought to sentimentalize his crucifixion less and emulate his message more—that there are values worth dying for and that often the struggle between values will be found in one's work world.[2]

A minister was discussing with a business audience the ethical dimensions of a certain course of action in business. When he opened the meeting for questions and responses, one person rose to his feet and said, "I've been listening to your ideas about how faith needs to influence how we live at work. I've been thinking, too, about the cost if I were to put those ideas into practice. What I'm wondering is whether I can afford that much Christianity. I'm not sure I can."

Contrast that comment with how Dave Thomas, founder of Wendy's, responded when asked in a television interview what characterized successful people he had observed in various walks of life. He replied: they are God-loving, they are honest, and they help others. They put others first and themselves second.[3]

Christians in biblical times also faced challenging ethical choices as they sought to live out their faith at work. For example, Revelation 2:18-28 records a message to the church of Thyatira. At least part of the context for the condemnation of the church's toleration of evil may well have related to members' behavior at work.

Thyatira was a trading center, and numerous trade guilds flourished there. Social meals dedicated to pagan deities were part of the life of such guilds. All who participated in the trading life of the city would have found it advantageous if not necessary to participate fully in a trade guild, including the social meals.[4] Could Christians participate?

Paul dealt with a similar issue in 1 Corinthians 8, where he counseled strong Christians to avoid actions that might bring harm to weaker Christians if weaker Christians were led to participate by their example and become ensnared in evil. The situation at Thyatira may have involved an even more sinister form of paganism. The passage in Revelation condemns tolerating "that woman Jezebel."

This condemnation of behavior that reached into the world of work would have challenged the Christians at Thyatira. How would they be able to maintain their Christian ethical commitments while they sought to get ahead, or just survive economically, in a business world that tempted them toward another style of life? Could they afford that much Christianity?

Difficulties People of Faith Face

Almost all businesses operate by standards of ethical behavior. These standards may be high and comprehensive, or low and limited.

Corporate policy manuals generally deal with certain ethical expectations of the corporation and of its employees. The policies speak to such issues as whether acceptance of gifts from suppliers or customers is permitted, what types of behavior are prohibited, which situations involve conflicts of interest to avoid, and what standards of honesty the corporation demands.

Government employees have a similar set of standards to follow. In August, 1992, for example, the Office of Government Ethics published *Standards of Ethical Conduct for Employees of the Executive Branch*. These rules deal with gifts from outside sources, gifts between employees, conflicting financial interests, misuse of one's position for private gain, and use of government property for unauthorized purposes.

For people of faith to violate the ethical standards of their employers would be unthinkable and without justification, since these
standards usually are based on the most basic understandings of ethical
behavior. Note, however, such corporate and governmental standards
often refer mainly to financial dealings. While being above reproach in
one's financial dealings is an important part of business ethics, the
ethical issues workers—including Christian workers—face are far
broader than financial concerns alone.

Ethics in business includes financial matters, but it also involves
how people behave—or ought to behave—toward one another in all
their relationships.[5] Biblical teachings as well as current books and
courses on business ethics recognize this important truth, but it
evidently has not yet trickled down—or, better, up—to practical
perceptions about business ethics.

Hart and Krueger's study of how Christians apply their faith to
their work reported that survey participants had ethical problems with
such matters as these: "termination of employees, discrimination
against women and minorities, and organizational pressure to make
unrealistic promises."[6] The first two items ordinarily are spoken to in
corporate policies, but that does not mean employees believe there are
no difficulties involved in how the corporation applies these policies.
Indeed, employees may question the ethics of the organization's termination policies, and they certainly may be aware of undercurrents of
racism and sexism in spite of official corporate policy. Even Christians
can have serious blind spots in all of these areas. If they do, like new-
born kittens they need to grow up and have their eyes opened.

The third item in the list of concerns, organizational pressure, is a
part of life in almost every organization—including religious organizations and other organizations with noble purposes. People of faith
ask themselves—as well they should and must—how far they can go
to be "good soldiers" in the corporate army without losing their souls
or being a part of a corporate action they believe to be unethical. Will
they have to sell their souls to make their numbers—the numbers the
corporation believes are important?

The preceding paragraph does not intend to indict all of the business world for unethical practices. Indeed, as a highly successful
business leader reminded me, trust is a vital part of doing business.
Dave Thomas stated, "Honesty and integrity are your most important
assets."[7]

Still, pressures to be unethical are subtle but real in all organizations, including business organizations. In fact, the subtlety of organizational pressure makes it all the more powerful.

People at various levels of an organization have differing views of ethical behavior in the organization. Research shows that the lower employees are on the corporate ladder, the more pressure they feel from the top of the organization to act unethically in order to keep their jobs. In one study, 64% of the respondents agreed that managers felt pressure to compromise moral values as they did their work.

This figure is challenging enough, but a closer look at the responses reveals areas of even greater concern. The pattern of the responses was quite different for top, middle, and lower management. Only 50% of top management felt pressure to compromise their moral values. For middle management, though, the percentage rose to 65%. Meanwhile, 85% of lower-level management felt organizational pressure to compromise their ethical convictions.[8]

What do you suppose could be the reason for these differences in perceptions of organizational pressure to go against one's ethical commitments? An obvious possible explanation for the differing perceptions at varying levels in the organization is that the farther up the organization one goes, the less ethical are the people. If you're in top or middle management, you probably won't like this suggestion, but could it be so, like it or not? Before dismissing such a conclusion out of hand as being an unfair attack, top and middle management needs to ask what signals they give to people they supervise that would lead to such a disparity in ethical perceptions at various levels in the organization.

This broader understanding of ethical living certainly increases the range of ethical difficulty that people of faith face as they seek to live faith's values at work. An additional source of difficulty is that almost every aspect of ethical living contains some gray areas. Furthermore, every business culture contains its own unwritten set of understandings about how much variation in ethical behavior is proper and how much is improper in these gray areas.

For example, should you *ever* use the office copy machine for personal use? How many copies do you have to make for yourself or your external organization before you cross the line into improper ethical behavior? One? Two? Ten? A hundred?

Even people of faith can find themselves using one of several common justifications for actions in the gray areas. These justifications include:

- Everyone—or everyone at my level—does it.
- The company won't miss it.
- They really owe it to me.
- It's not really illegal or immoral, after all.
- It's in the best interests of the business.
- No one will find out.
- Since I'm helping the company, the company will stand behind me.
- I had no other choice.
- I broke the rules just this once.
- This is really an unselfish thing to do, since it will make more money for our customers, keep the shareholders happy, and keep our workers employed.
- It's the easiest way we can think of to get the job done.
- I'm not convinced that doing the right thing really works out in the long run.
- It's such a small matter.
- People around here do lots worse things than this.[9]

Do any of these justifications sound familiar? Take a look at them again. They're really rationalizations, not justifications; excuses, not reasons. Anytime one of them comes to mind when you are contemplating a decision or action, beware.

Practical Ways of Approaching Ethical Decisions and Actions

Because justifying our actions is so easy, most of us need considerable help in deciding how we will respond to the ethical issues we face at work. The next section offers a foundation for deciding and responding as we face ethical issues, both obvious and subtle, gray as well as black-and-white.

Resolve to make the ethical choice in every situation.

A legendary story about Winston Churchill has him seated next to a pretty young thing at a banquet. She was intent on getting ahead in life in any way possible. Knowing of her reputation, Churchill asked, "Would you marry a man for a million dollars?" She replied, "Why, yes, I would." Churchill then asked, "Would you marry him for $100?" She replied with indignation, "Of course not! What sort of person do you think I am?" He is said to have replied, "My dear, we've already established that. We're just now trying to establish the degree."

Of course, plenty of people other than her have also established what sort of people they are, and they often act accordingly. People of various ages and both genders have decided they are willing to sell themselves to get lots of things that are important to them—including the security, advancement, and money their jobs provide.

People of faith will not be able to live as people of faith at work or anywhere else with such an approach to ethical issues, however. The beginning point for responding positively to ethical challenges is to decide at the beginning that you will be an ethical person and that every decision and action will be entirely ethical as far as you know how to make it so, whatever the cost to you personally. In other words, in every decision and action, you will make your faith commitment primary, not secondary, whatever factors are involved in the decision or action considered. To whatever extent you are able to see love for God and love for neighbor involved in a decision or action, you will act accordingly.

Ethical behavior is not the dessert to be added to the meal or left off at a whim. Rather it is the main course of life, including life at work. With such a base for decisions and actions, you may evaluate certain situations wrongly, make wrong decisions, and take wrong actions, of course. You'll still make mistakes. The likelihood of your doing so, however, is infinitesimally smaller than if your ethical life were on a shakier foundation.

Thomas Merton wrote:

> The real meaning of faith is *the rejection of everything that is not Christ in order that all life, all truth, all hope, all reality may be sought and found "in Christ."*[10]

Such single-minded commitment is demanded if we are to respond positively to the varieties of ethical choices that confront us as people of faith in the world of work.

This sort of single-minded, bedrock commitment is encompassed in Jesus' instructions to his disciples as he explained to them the nature of his ministry. He said,

> If any want to become my followers, let them deny themselves and take up their cross and follow me. For those who want to save their life will lose it, and those who lose their life for my sake, and for the sake of the gospel, will save it. For what will it profit them to gain the whole world and forfeit their life. (Mark 8:34-36)

We often are as bewildered and slow in understanding and taking these words to heart as the disciples were. The words do remind us, though, of the need for a radical, bedrock decision about the kind of people we will be, including when we are at work.

Integrity describes the kind of ethical decision making and behavior demanded. Integrity has to do with a basic honesty about one's representations of what truth is and what one's values are. Integrity calls for making decisions and actions consistent with one's words.

The word *integrity* is rooted in the word *integer,* meaning "one." The idea implied is, a person of integrity is a person who is *one* person, not two or more, in the way he or she decides and acts. In the currently popular way of describing integrity, integrity calls for both "talking the talk" and "walking the talk." The *acts* of a person of integrity are at one with the person's *being,* with who he or she *is.* The message is: "Keep your heart with all vigilance, for from it flow the springs of life" (Prov 4:23).

A magazine reporter asked Joseph Juran, the noted expert on quality in business, his recipe for a good life. Juran was in his late eighties and could look back on a lifetime of contributions to the business world. While demurring that he was not an expert on such a recipe, he mentioned that one of the important ingredients was this: "Live a life of integrity; you're at peace with yourself."[11]

Integrity is based on the decision about what kind of person you are and will be. This decision is then played out in the countless decisions and acts—large, small, and in-between. The beginning is the choice, though, to *be* a person of integrity. If you want to face ethical issues as a person of faith, resolve to be a person of integrity as you face every one of them. Be proactive in seeking to make the ethical choice willingly and eagerly instead of reluctantly.

What this also means is that businesses and individuals within businesses must adopt a different standard of measurement for success than the bottom line. If making a profit is the sole or dominant goal of the business, then I can guarantee that at some point the business will make the wrong ethical decision. One study on illegal behavior in business found that the concern for profits was the number-one work pressure faced by middle managers. Ninety percent of those who responded to the study believed that such pressure led to unethical behavior.[12] I believe the 90% are right 100% of the time on that matter.

I can hear the protest: What other goal for business is there than profit? How about, delivering value to the customer? Successful, ethical business leaders focus on customers. They provide products and services of value to their customers, to meet their customers' needs; they also recognize that their employees will not be able to meet their customers' needs if employees' needs are not met as well.

For such business leaders, honesty is indeed the best policy, not a pretty good policy ordinarily, providing one can make a profit at the same time. It is the best policy because it is the right policy, in line with their values. Too, it is in line with their values because it results in right treatment of people, customers and employees alike.

This approach puts ethical behavior in the pragmatic context of the marketplace, not merely of idealistic philanthropy. Ethical decisions and actions become not just what one should do if one can afford it in given situations, but what one should do because it is at the heart of what positive human activity is all about.

Be scrupulously honest in every area of your work.

It should go without saying, shouldn't it? But it doesn't. The temptations to be less than honest are often so great and the rationalizations often seem to us so plausible that it must be said: People of faith should be scrupulously honest in every area of their work life.

If you're ever tempted to engage in something that seems small and yet even slightly shady, reject the temptation immediately. In expense reports, for instance, it's best to pay money out of your own pocket if your putting an item on your expense report would raise even the slightest question. Why allow such a small matter to cast doubt on your reputation for integrity? If you find in your possession so much as a pencil that you know belongs not to you but to your employer, give it back. Clear enough? With honesty in such minute matters, one obviously ought to be forthright and honest, with no deception, in all the larger issues of business.

Christians should be known as people of finely-tuned, ultra-scrupulous honesty—regarding their own actions rather than merely in judgment of others' actions, I might add. No amount of talk about faith can overcome the failure to walk one's faith in the area of honesty.

It's hard to tell whether all the stories told about Abraham Lincoln actually happened and whether he actually said all the things he's reputed to have said. Nevertheless, a story I heard about him affected me profoundly as a child. The story, which I take as being true, is that when Lincoln was a young man, he worked for a time as a clerk in a dry goods store. One day he realized he had overcharged a customer— by one penny. What did Lincoln do? Keep the penny? After all, his employer likely would never find out. Lincoln, though, walked two miles through the snow to return the penny to the customer. Of course, a penny is worth a whole lot less these days! But isn't the principle still the same?

In Titus 2:9, Paul orders Christian slaves "not to pilfer, but to show complete and perfect fidelity, so that in everything they may be an ornament to the doctrine of God our Savior." While these Christians could perhaps have rationalized stealing because of their dehumanized state as slaves, Paul insisted on complete honesty for the sake of bringing honor and not dishonor to Christ. The quality of complete, scrupulous honesty is still an essential for people of faith in the world of work today.

Being scrupulously honest includes, of course, working hard at your job. With biting humor, Proverbs 10:26 describes a lazy employee like this: "Like vinegar to the teeth and smoke to the eyes, so are the lazy to their employers."

We know little about Jesus' life as a worker, but we do know that he was indeed a worker—a carpenter. Can we imagine him being a lazy, dishonest carpenter? Or can we think of him running a contracting business that cut corners in order to line his pockets or even just to keep his business afloat? Paul admonished Christians who were slaves,

> Slaves, obey your earthly masters in everything, not only while being watched and in order to please them, but wholeheartedly, fearing the Lord. Whatever your task, put yourselves into it, as done for the Lord and not for your masters, since you know that from the Lord you will receive the inheritance as your reward; you serve the Lord Christ. (Col 3:22-24)

Apply some critical tests to your decisions and actions.

Jesus summarized the law in two brief commandments. He said we are to love God with our whole selves and love our neighbor as we love ourselves (Mark 12:28-34). These two brief commandments are really all we need to test our decisions and actions for their ethical soundness and appropriateness, even in the world of business.

But plenty of decisions come our way in a given week at work in which we wonder how we can practically, specifically, apply the principles of love of God and neighbor to the knotty problems we face. Such quandaries are experienced by people at all levels in a corporation as they seek to live out their faith. They wonder how, in the concrete world of business, people of faith live out this admonition to love God and neighbor. The fact is, both God and neighbor often seem far removed from the spreadsheets and line management, machinery and meetings that many people of faith face at work every day. Neither God nor neighbor seems anywhere close.

In fact, business and individuals within business sometimes tend to operate as if love of God and neighbor has no place in the realm of commerce. Even to talk of loving God and neighbor in the business world may seem far-fetched, certainly in any practical sense. Right and wrong may be discussed as business plans are made and actions contemplated, but the debate may be more in terms of public relations than of higher standards.

Indeed, in a statement that has become something of a caricature of this approach to business, economist Milton Friedman asserted that making as much money as possible for the company's shareholders is the only social responsibility of corporate officials.[13] To be fair, I must note that Friedman qualified his statement by putting it in a framework of various moral responsibilities.[14] Still, in practice, some have taken his statement as license for making money take precedence over all other concerns in business, including ethics.

No sensible person would argue that profit has its place in the world of business. The larger questions are how much of a place and at what price. The approach to business that holds the importance of the bottom line only leads to a business culture that often pressures individuals to disregard or at least sublimate ethical behavior in order to support the company's supreme goal of making money.

In such a business culture, people of faith need guidance and help in making ethical choices that reflect their faith rather than ignore it. They need help in identifying what exactly people look like at work when they are loving God and neighbor, especially when they are deciding and behaving ethically. They wonder what sort of tests can be applied to determine whether a specific decision or action truly honors God and shows love to one's fellow human beings.

Max DePree, CEO of a furniture manufacturer known for its ethics and quality as well as its profitableness, reminds us, "Organizations do not live on earnings alone."[15] Such a statement is more in line with biblical admonitions about money than is the business approach that makes the bottom line the sole, even dominant, value of business. Biblical passages such as Leviticus 19:9-10; Isaiah 58:3; Jeremiah 22:13; Hebrews 13:5; and James 4:13, 5:1-6 call for attention to issues other than money and profits.

Therefore, I want to suggest to you five questions you can ask to assist you in ethical decision making at work, decision making that shows love for God and one's fellow human beings. These questions apply at whatever level in the organization you find yourself or aspire to. All five of these questions need to be considered, not just one or

two or three or even four.[16] They offer guidance in dealing with the
more difficult ethical issues when we do not know immediately what
the proper ethical action is as well as with those actions when we know
what is right but are tempted to do something else.

(1) *Does the action or decision break the law, go against company
policy, or violate the code of ethics of your profession?* If the answer to
any part of this question is anything other than a firm No, then you
may be about to become involved in unethical behavior, behavior that
fails to show love for God and one's neighbor.

Of course, items that are legal, within company policy, or in line
with your profession's code of ethics are not necessarily ethical. I grew
up, for example, in a society in which racial segregation was ordered
by law and racial discrimination was perfectly legal, but such behavior
was not at all ethical. In the same manner, just because an action is
company policy does not mean it is morally right. Company policy
may be written or applied in such a way as to justify unethical behavior on the part of the people who make and apply the policy. Even the
code of ethics in your profession can be blind to ethical realities.
Therefore, simply following the law, staying within company policy,
and abiding by the code of ethics of one's profession do not necessarily result in ethical behavior. In fact, going against any of these
entities—law, policy, or code of ethics—may be the most ethical
decision and action one can take.

Nevertheless, any action that appears to violate a law, a policy, or
an item in a code of ethics should be considered with the utmost care.
If we choose to act contrary to any of them, we should be prepared to
have a penalty exacted. At their best, laws, policies, and codes of ethics
represent accumulated and tested wisdom concerning the best and
fairest ways of acting. While people of faith have on occasion found it
necessary to refuse to follow such accepted rules (see Acts 5:29), they
will more often find them helpful guides to ethical behavior, especially
when considered along with the remaining four elements of ethical
decision making.

(2) *Does the action or decision anyone?* The motto of the physician is, "Do no harm." This is a good principle to follow in the larger
world of work, too. If an action we are contemplating brings harm to
someone, anyone, we should ponder carefully the decision's ethical
dimensions. At least one writer in the field of business ethics considers
this the foundational question to be answered in considering whether a
decision or action is ethical.[17]

A plant being relocated may bring harm to the community in
which it currently resides. A department reorganization may bring

harm to individuals within the department. Should an action be taken, then, that brings harm to the community or the individuals involved? Perhaps the answer is still Yes, but how the relocation or the reorganization is done and with what consideration for the people involved may need to be thought through carefully in light of the ethical considerations raised by this question.

A well-known company found that its baby oil could be used quite successfully as a product for helping people have a "healthy tan." This was before the current public realization that tanning is not good for one's health. The product manager saw this new use as a great avenue for expanding the sales of this particular product. He brought the idea to the company's executive committee. There, however, one participant mentioned the concern then developing in the medical community about the harmful effects of tanning. As a result, even though millions of dollars were at stake annually, the company decided that it could not promote a product's use in a manner that ultimately would do harm to people or at least encourage them to do harm to themselves.[18] The approach of this company, Johnson & Johnson, stands in sharp contrast to that of the tobacco companies, doesn't it?

(3) *Does the action or decision help people?* How? One person of faith remarked that his work essentially was to make military weapons with which to kill people. He said he felt some concern about his participation in that activity even though it was on behalf of the military. The work was legal, but he wondered whether it actually brought good by helping people. Of course, it's possible to justify such an occupation as actually helping people even though weapons of destruction are being created. We live in an unsafe, unstable world in which the strong do not always act for the common good, to say the least. The restraining force of military power sometimes seems useful, even necessary, in order to provide for the defense of the common good. But if we can't understand how such a decision or action actually helps, it's cause for concern and reflection about the ethics of the matter.

Even if you are involved in producing a product or service that does clearly help people, it's still important that you ask the question, "To what extent do my individual actions help people?" The goal should be to use your position of employment and the myriad decisions and actions connected with it to behave in ways that help people. Never use a position of privilege, however small it may be, to take advantage of any person.

The word of the Lord through the prophet Zechariah is as applicable to the world of work as to all other human endeavor: "Render true judgments, show kindness and mercy to one another" (7:9). We must be concerned about doing good for people as well as avoiding doing harm to them. Note, this verse has no "except" clause in it. It doesn't say "except if you're the CEO," or "except if you're in management," or "except if you're in sales," or "except if you're at work, of course."

Tom Chappell asks, "We expect priests and teachers, artists and naturalists, to care for and celebrate the human spirit. Shouldn't we expect the same from CEOs?"[19] Well, shouldn't we? And from other top managers, middle managers, first-line supervisors, and employees? Why not, pray tell?

(4) *Does the action or decision result in fairness and balance among all the stakeholders in the matter?* The concept of stakeholders in addition to shareholders has come into ethical discussions in recent years as a way of recognizing that a business's actions affect more individuals and groups than merely its owners or management.

Who are the stakeholders in a business? The owners and shareholders, to be sure. But employees are also stakeholders, as is the general community. The company's customers are also stakeholders.[20] Each of these entities has a stake in the decisions and actions of the company and should be considered in deliberations about ethics.

Does this approach sound idealistic, even simplistic? Recent research indicates that companies that value *all* their stakeholders—not just their shareholders—outperform financially those companies that put only their shareholders first. In other words, companies that *don't* put their shareholders first do better for their shareholders than companies that put *only* their shareholders first.[21] Another study identified companies that had a set of written principles stating that service to the public was their central mission and that had followed these principles for at least a generation. The return to shareholders for this group of fifteen companies was more than seven times the return of the typical company on the Dow Jones list over the most recent thirty-year period.[22]

A senior manager of a major company known for its ethical commitments described the company's concern for all of its stakeholders as being like trying to juggle four balls at the same time. Imagine, he suggested, that the balls for customer, employees, and the community are white and the one for the shareholders is red. If one drops the red ball, the game is over, but one must still give careful attention to the white ones and not slight them.[23]

If you're not responsible for the welfare of an entire company and supervise no one but yourself, do you have other stakeholders in your decisions and actions than your supervisor who represents the company who pays you a salary? Certainly you do. Your fellow employees are in a sense stakeholders as is the ultimate customer for your labors. While responding to pressures and acting unethically might for a time satisfy the stakeholder who pays your salary, you might at the same time be treating unfairly and unethically these other stakeholders. If a company's requested action is unfair toward one's fellow employees, the person who lives by the values of faith needs to find the courage to act ethically in spite of the company's demands. Any company worth working for will want to have ethical employees and will provide ways for ethical concerns to be expressed and resolved. Is there a risk? Of course, but who said this was going to be easy or safe?

(5) *Is the action or decision something about which you would be unashamed, even proud, for others to know?* What others, especially those dearest to us, would think of us if they knew of our actions is exceedingly worth considering. Would your child, for example, be glad to know that you had acted in such a manner as you might be debating? A concern for secrecy often signals a concern about ethics.

A lack of a sense of guilt does *not* indicate guiltlessness, however. We can teach our consciences to overlook wrong acts in ourselves. As Proverbs warns, "All one's ways may be pure in one's own eyes, but the Lord weighs the spirit" (16:2).

Moving beyond family and friends to business relationships, the reality is that the trust others have in you may be your most significant asset. Lose it and you've lost everything, regardless of your technical competence and whatever you may gain in the long term. If the thought is, "just this once won't be so bad," then ask yourself what your taking this certain action or making this certain decision ten times would do to the trust others have in you.

Along these same lines, it's also worth asking yourself this question, which may appear crass but instead is a real-life issue: How will this action appear when the opposing attorney describes it in court? Any person with much experience in business recognizes that this possibility is not at all a fantasy. It happens to someone every day; maybe it's happened to you. The answer? To the best of your ability, always decide and act in ways that will make your actions be above reproach when others learn of them.

The greater your position of leadership and management, accept even greater responsibility for living by faith's values.

A 1992 survey conducted by *Industry Week* reveals that 87 percent of employees believe it is very important for management to be ethical.

This is good news. The bad news is, less than half of that number—39 percent—believe management *is* ethical.[24]

How ironic—and how disturbing—that top management may see themselves as the guardians of the ethical life of the corporation, while lower level employees see top management as the least ethical and as the people who pressure them to make ethical compromises. All employees at whatever level need to be aware of and resistant to pressures to compromise their convictions, of course, but top-level managers have the additional challenge of evaluating how their actions and policies may affect the moral sensitivities of people lower in the organization. The responsibilities of leadership include that obligation.

Leaders need the vision and courage to consider their actions and decisions through the eyes of their followers, including lower-level employees. As Max DePree states so wisely and eloquently, "The open demonstration of integrity is essential; followers must be wholeheartedly convinced of their leaders' integrity."[25] Leaders must be ready and willing to be "ruthlessly honest."[26] Any slip, real or perceived to be real by others in the organization, can seriously damage one's leadership ability, the organization itself, and the ethical dimensions of individual employees' lives.

If you are a manager, you may feel insulted that employees below you would question your integrity. You may right now be thinking of explanations for employees' opinions, such as jealousy.

Reasons exist, however, for this impression employees have. These reasons can be found in the unethical actions and decisions that employees in almost every company observe management making. If you are a manager, and particularly if you are a manager determined to live by the values of your faith, you must be careful to live so as to change that impression.

A prominent expert on business management, Warren Bennis, stated the issue well when he wrote:

> Every organization tempts its leaders to become preoccupied with the priorities of the moment at the cost of ignoring the overarching questions that determine the quality of all our lives, such questions as: Is this right? Is it good for our children? Is it good for the planet?[27]

You are not exempt from this temptation, but you are in an excellent position to resist it. If you will live by the values of your faith, you have the potential for changing the focus of your organization from the merely urgent to the truly important.

Max DePree states, "Integrity is the linchpin of leadership. . . . Behavior is the only score that's kept. Lose integrity, and a leader will find herself in a directionless organization going nowhere."[28]

From a purely business standpoint, ethical living is important and essential for leadership and management. In cases of sexual harassment, for example, the law holds managers especially responsible for preventing and stopping sexual harassment between employees. If the law attributes this level of importance to the actions of management, certainly one's faith should call for added responsibility by managers in all ethical issues.

When Moses' father-in-law Jethro advised him about management and organization, Jethro urged Moses to seek out specially qualified people to assist Moses in the task of managing the affairs of the Hebrews. These people were to be people "who fear God, are trustworthy, and hate dishonest gain" (Exod 18:21). Honesty was an absolute essential for this important job. The highest of ethical standards is still called for on the part of those who manage and lead today.

The Importance of Living by Faith's Values

A highly successful commercial real estate agent who seeks to live his faith said that when he was engaged in a business transaction and the other party mentioned that he or she attended a certain church, he was never sure what effect that statement would have on the manner in which the business deal was conducted. He could not be sure whether the person would actually live by his faith's values. In fact, many such experiences had led him to treat such a statement as a tip-off to be extra careful. That's sad, isn't it? Unfortunately, that's the real world.

On the other hand, another successful real estate agent said he could have made a lot more money if he had not wanted to get a good night's sleep every night. He preferred being ethical to staying awake planning a shady deal or worrying about one he had just completed. (Wouldn't it be good if these two real estate agents could do deals together! Or at least for each of them to be certain that the person with whom they were dealing had the same high standards of ethical behavior? It would make life a lot simpler and more enjoyable for everybody.)

Ethical behavior in business is important. In a recent study more than fifteen hundred executives from twenty countries identified personal ethics as the most important characteristic needed in the ideal CEO.[29] Ethical behavior in business is even more important for people of faith, if that's possible. Living by faith's values at work is evidence to us and others that our faith is real, real enough to affect our everyday lives. Ethical behavior at work is a way of living out our recognition that we are accountable for our actions throughout eternity, not just past the next financial report of the corporation or the next paycheck.

Actually, values, not money, are the true bottom line of any organization. Many who work in large organizations can resonate with this statement from management consultant John Cowan: "After years of working in a bureaucracy, I am convinced that the absence of character is the cancer of organizations."[30]

Decisions and actions based on values are more important in the long term to a company's well-being than is a positive quarterly financial report. People of faith who live by their values function as the preventative medicine that keeps organizations healthy and as the curative medicine that enables organizations to get well when they get sick.

Notes

[1]James A. Autry, *Life and Work: A Manager's Search for Meaning* (New York: William Morrow & Co., Inc., 1994) 100-101.

[2]Matthew Fox, *The Reinvention of Work: A New Vision of Livelihood for Our Time* (San Francisco: HarperSanFrancisco, 1994) 13.

[3]Interview with Tom Snyder on CNBC, November 1994.

[4]George Eldon Ladd, *A Commentary on the Revelation of John* (Grand Rapids MI: Eerdmans, 1972) 50.

[5]See William D. Hall, *Making the Right Decision: Ethics for Managers* (New York: John Wiley & Sons, Inc., 1993) 40.

[6]Stephen Hart and David A. Krueger, *Faith and Work: Personal Needs and Congregational Responses,* The Center for Ethics and Corporate Policy's Congregations and Business Life Project, final report (Chicago: The Center for Ethics and Corporate Policy, 1991) 6.

[7]R. David Thomas, "How to Add by Subtracting," *Higher Than the Top* (Nashville TN: Dimensions for Living, 1993) 86.

[8]Tad Tuleja, *Beyond the Bottom Line: How Business Leaders Are Turning Principles into Profits* (New York: Facts on File Publications, 1985) 170.

[9]Adapted and expanded from Tuleja, 45-48; Saul W. Gellerman, "Why 'Good' Managers Make Bad Ethical Choices," in *Ethics in Practice: Managing the Moral Corporation,* ed., with an introduction by Kenneth R. Andrews (Boston: Harvard Business School Press, 1989) 22; and Charles E. Watson, *Managing with Integrity: Insights from America's CEOs,* foreword by C. William Verity (New York: Praeger, 1991) 55-56.

[10]Thomas Merton, *Life and Holiness* (New York: Doubleday, 1963) 78, italics in original.

[11]Joseph Juran, quoted in Barbara Ettore, "Juran on Quality," *Management Review* (January 1994): 11.

[12]Laura L. Nash, *Good Intentions Aside: A Manager's Guide to Resolving Ethical Problems* (Boston: Harvard Business School Press, 1990) 135, citing Marshall B. Clinard, *Corporate Ethics and Crime: The Role of Middle Management* (Beverly Hills CA: Sage Publications, 1983) 91-95.

[13]Milton Friedman, *Capitalism and Freedom* (Chicago: University of Chicago Press, 1962) 133.

[14]Michael Novak, *Business as a Calling: Work and the Examined Life* (New York: The Free Press, 1996) 141.

[15]Max DePree, *Leadership Jazz* (New York: Dell Publishing, 1992) 39.

[16]The first, fourth, and fifth questions are adapted from Kenneth Blanchard and Norman Vincent Peale, *The Power of Ethical Management* (New York: William Morrow & Co., Inc., 1988) 27.

[17]Hall, 116.

[18]Nash, 83-85.

[19]Tom Chappell, *The Soul of a Business: Managing for Profit and the Common Good* (New York: Bantam Books, 1993) xv-xvi.

[20]Arnold Brown and Edith Weiner, *Supermanaging: How to Harness Change for Personal and Organizational Success* (New York: McGraw-Hill, 1984) 197.

[21]Robert H. Waterman, Jr., *What America Does Right* (New York: W. W. Norton & Co., 1994) 26, citing John P. Kotter and James L. Heskett, *Corporate Culture and Performance* (New York: The Free Press, 1992) 11.

[22]Waterman, 297-298, citing James E. Burke, "The Leverage of Goodwill," speech to the Advertising Council, 16 November 1993, 2.

[23]Tuleja, 31.

[24]Frank S. Sonnenberg, "The Age of Intangibles," *Management Review* (January 1994):52.

[25]DePree, 10.

[26]Ibid., 24.

[27]Warren Bennis, *An Invented Life: Reflections on Leadership and Change,* foreword by Tom Peters (Reading MA: Addison-Wesley, 1993) xv.

[28]DePree, 220.

[29]Nash, 7, citing Korn/Ferry International and Columbia University Graduate School of Business, *21st Century Report: Reinventing the CEO* (Los Angeles, 1989) 41.

[30]John Cowan, *Small Decencies: Reflections and Meditations on Being Human in the Workplace* (New York: HarperBusiness, 1992) 92.

Chapter 6
Look for Faith's Meaning in Daily Work

What do people want from their work? In his bestselling book on business leadership, Stephen Covey puts it this way:

> Meaning is the challenging need of the modern worker. It's not enough to work to eat or stay on the job because you're treated well. Nor is it enough to have an opportunity to contribute your talents and to unleash some of your potential. People want to know why.[1]

People who seek to approach their work and all of life from a faith perspective may feel the need for meaning even more keenly than this dramatic statement indicates. They want to know the meaning of their daily work in relation to their faith as well as to know work's meaning in general. Finding the answer is often far from easy.

The Problem

So what's the problem? Ernst Friedrich Schumacher, a proponent of a more humane and Christian approach to work and business, states the problem by suggesting that our society's approach to structuring jobs tends to make

> most forms of work—manual and white-collared—utterly uninteresting and meaningless. Mechanical, artificial, divorced from nature, utilizing only the smallest part of man's potential capabilities, it sentences the great majority of workers to spending their working lives in a way which contains no worthy challenge, no stimulus to self-perfection, chance of development, no element of Beauty, Truth, or Goodness. The basic aim of modern industrialism is not to make work satisfying but to raise productivity.[2]

The only people who could find much fault with Schumacher's analysis would be of two sorts: (1) the idealists who have been sheltered completely from the harsh realities of the world of everyday work and (2) the fortunate few who have been able to so structure their work—or have it so structured for them—that they somehow, almost miraculously, have risen above the deadening approach Schumacher pictured.

The way Schumacher described it is the way it all too often is in the world of work. Any exceptions someone might cite are just that— exceptions to the norm. Work for many is often deadening, with little obvious meaning. Many people of faith have these sorts of jobs and experience the resulting meaninglessness, too.

Attempts at Solutions

As people of faith experience the same vexing problem of meaning-lessness in their work, they also often seek to solve the problem in the same manner that other workers do when they are unable to find meaning in their work. They sentence themselves to a life term in their work and separate their work from the rest of their lives. They isolate themselves from attempts to find meaning at work and focus on pursuits beyond work as the source of meaning for their lives.

They may seek such meaning in recreation, hobbies, family activities, and even religious pursuits. They may see their work's meaning as enshrined only in their paycheck. Tragically, each day when they go to work, however, they enter the twilight world of non-meaning while on the job. There has to be a better way. Here are some practical ways by which people of faith can add meaning to their work itself.

Make Helping People the Goal of Work

Because love for and service to other people is so central to faith, this word of instruction is also the key to finding faith's meaning in one's work. Recognizing the meaning of work from the perspective of faith calls for seeing work as a way of helping people, directly and indirectly, including producing good products and services that help people.

New Testament interpreter G. Agrell suggests that the words in Ephesians 4:28 about a person's "working with his own hands" should be understood to mean "making a good product."[3] Although this interpretation might or might not be the most appropriate one, the idea certainly has merit. People of faith obviously should not be in the business of producing bad products and services. Such bad products and services would include both the products and services that are harmful to people as well as the products and services that could potentially be useful to people if their poor quality did not render them useless or even harmful. Rather, the products people of faith produce and the services they provide should be helpful to people.

The spirit of service is at the heart of the Christian faith. As Jesus said to the two disciples who sought greatness, "Whoever wishes to become great among you must be your servant" (Mark 10:43). Of course, Jesus demonstrated in his own life the meaning of being a servant. When he washed the feet of his disciples, he reminded them, "I have set you an example, that you also should do as I have done to you" (John 13:15).

Christians are familiar with hearing service talked about and with being challenged to demonstrate their faith through their service. Most often, the list of settings for such service includes the church property and church activities, the home, perhaps one's community, and the vague location of life in general. The work setting as an arena for service is often overlooked.

Should faith's emphasis on service stop at the door of entrance to the office or factory, though? Is service a concern of faith only at the place of worship or at one's home, in all the settings of life except work? Of course not.

The obligation and opportunity of Christian service continues at the office or factory and in the work of the office or factory itself, not just while one is on break or at lunch. People of faith can enhance their sense of meaning in their daily work if they will reclaim for their jobs themselves the emphasis on service that is intrinsic to faith.

The result will be not only an enhanced sense of meaning in work for the person but also a greater degree of effectiveness in the work itself. The current marketplace clamors for service, whether that be perceived as service to external customers—the people who actually buy the company's products—or internal customers—the coworkers down the line who depend on you to do your work well so they can do their work well. More than one used-to-be business establishment would still be in business or would be more profitable if it had seen service as not just company policy but company action.

My involvement with customer satisfaction efforts and total quality management has made me become quite sensitive, sometimes unfortunately, to the level of service I receive. Hardly anything is more offensive to me in a business transaction than to receive poor service at the same time I'm looking at a framed plaque of the company's mission statement that says the customer comes first. It's happened.

People who see their jobs as an opportunity to help people get what they need—whether coworkers or customers—and who go beyond what's expected to be of help are valued assets to any business. Making helping people one's goal on the job results in a win-win situation for employees as well as the employer. Employees receive greater meaning in their work, and their employer receives the benefits of having employees whose emphasis on helping other people cannot but make the company more successful.

These attitudes and actions of helpfulness and service are important in individual relationships, of course. They need to be extended beyond individual relationships, however.

In his classic book, *Servant Leadership,* Robert K. Greenleaf, who was an executive at a Fortune 500 company, advocated convincingly the need for leaders to be characterized by care, helpfulness, and service. Because large institutions now are so important in our society, he said, these same qualities need to be lived out in and made effective within these large institutions. In other words, care, helpfulness, and service need to characterize these large institutions just as they need to characterize one's individual relationships. So corporations, government, universities, and churches—all institutions, whether profit or nonprofit—need to focus and conduct their mission with an emphasis on service. Greenleaf taught:

> If a better society is to be built, one that is more just and more loving, one that provides greater creative opportunity for its people, then the most open course is to *raise both the capacity to serve and the very performance as servant* of existing institutions by new regenerative forces operating within them.[4]

With our society's emphasis on individualism, people of faith have tended to overlook or ignore the opportunities they have to influence institutions, not just individuals, toward good. Too, while they may have sought to serve other individuals at work, they have not seen with clarity the opportunities they have to influence toward servanthood the institutions of which they are a part. But the opportunities are available for leaders with vision who are concerned about influencing their institutions toward the service of people and society as a whole rather than serving only the company's bottom line.

Such a role for the person of faith within a large institution may call for the exercise of great wisdom and care, of course, for being "wise as serpents and innocent as doves" (Matt 10:16). But the opportunities are there.

The result of such an emphasis on service could bring good to many people and meaning to the person of faith as well. Again, Greenleaf points out the opportunities in this comment: "Servant-leaders are *healers* in the sense of *making whole* by helping others to a larger and nobler vision and purpose than they would be likely to attain for themselves."[5] Business, as every other area of life, is characterized too much by littleness, not largeness, of purpose. People of faith who take their servant role seriously can influence decisions and events toward an enlarged vision that takes account of more than the immediate bottom line. Such servants have opportunities to offer reminders in the most crass of business deals that books are kept in eternity as well as time. Ideally, they can create a climate through their influence that such business deals will not even come up for consideration.

Recognize the Value of Mundane Work

Seeing how some jobs actually help people is sometimes puzzling, of course. The mundane nature of the work may make it appear beneath us or at best fail to engage the best of our skills.

In a sense, however, the more mundane a job may appear, the more necessary and helpful to people it may actually be. Who, for example, would be missed more in a large city on a given day: the mayor, or the mail carrier who delivers your mail, or the garbage truck driver who picks up the garbage at your house and today is garbage pickup day? Who would be missed more at your office on a given day: the CEO or the person assigned to accomplish a specific task essential to a specific operation, perhaps the switchboard operator or the heating and cooling technician?

These questions are not meant to suggest that the mayor or the CEO do not perform useful functions. The questions are intended to affirm, however, that the mundane nature of a job should not be taken to mean that it is less helpful to people than are the more glamorous jobs that appear to have greater status.

People who have developed at least a minor degree of affluence and moved up in Maslow's scale of meaning to the extent that they give little concern to the source of their next meal should not forget that basic needs still have to be cared for. They should also recognize that those whose occupations provide for their basic needs deserve their thanks.

At a family gathering, adult granddaughters were working together in the kitchen along with their grandmother. The granddaughters began talking about the modern conveniences they appreciated most. One named the microwave and another the dishwasher. They named other conveniences as the grandmother listened but said nothing. Finally, one of the granddaughters attempted to involve the grandmother in the conversation and asked, "What modern convenience do you appreciate most, Grandmother?"

The grandmother replied, "Oh, I like all of those things you named, but I believe my favorite modern convenience is running water." As one whose chores as a boy included drawing water from the well, I can identify with and affirm the grandmother's answer!

Sometimes a disaster such as an earthquake or a flood is required to remind us that we depend for survival on people performing some work that seems rather mundane in more normal times. We want our water to be drinkable, we want food to be available, we want our garbage to be picked up, we want our electricity to work, we want the telephone to operate properly, we want the roads to be passable if not free of potholes, and we want to feel the security of living in an ordered society.

These and similar needs call for some rather mundane work to be done by someone. We do ourselves and the workers who do such work a disservice if we fail to recognize its value and indeed its necessity. Furthermore, people of faith who do such work would do well to see meaning in it and indeed to see it as an act of ministry and an expression of their calling. As Elton Trueblood wrote,

> It is part of our secular snobbery to feel that some work is respectable while other work lowers the social standing of a family. . . . If truck driving is needed to feed and clothe and house our people, then truck driving is noble and can be a holy calling.[6]

We too readily allow ourselves to be trapped into our culture's evaluations of work. American culture tends to believe that things associated with the body are not as valuable as things associated with the mind. Hence, blue-collar work is not valued by some people to the extent that white-collar work is valued. The reason? The assumption is, blue-collar people may have to exert their bodies' strength—in a manner similar to animals—and get their hands dirty; white-collar workers probably won't.[7]

Christians may allow this cultural prejudice to creep over into the area of meaning, suggesting that the work of the body provides less meaning than the work of the mind. This idea cannot be squared with the biblical view of work and of the people who do the work.

When I stopped at a local restaurant for breakfast, I found the parking lot filled mainly with pickup trucks and equipment vans. I had eaten there before, and so I knew what to expect besides good food. The restaurant was filled with people in work clothes plus a couple of police officers in uniform. Only a few ties were in sight. I do not romanticize the work my fellow restaurant-goers were on their way to do. It's important, though, that every person who dresses up to go to work values and respects the work of people who work with their hands as well as their minds. More than one of those folks dressed in jeans, T-shirt, and work boots wore a beeper, by the way!

In seeking to find meaning in work that seems mundane and ordinary, we would do well to recognize that the spiritual can and must be expressed through the material. Even God chose that way in which to express faith's message best. God sent Jesus as a baby—a baby who would grow up to work as a carpenter.

An additional way to find meaning in jobs that seem ordinary, mundane, and even routine is to consider how they actually help people. Certain occupations appear to be more directly helpful to people than others, of course. For example, we may be able to see clearly the opportunities for helping people that doctors, nurses, teachers, firefighters, police officers, emergency medical technicians, social workers, and people in related occupations have. The challenge is for people of faith to see meaning in jobs that appear not to be related to helping people. Some workers spend their days or nights performing tasks that appear to them to have meaning only as the means by which they get their paycheck. Office or factory jobs, for example, that are a substantial distance from the end consumer may appear to lack meaning. Where is the meaning in such jobs anyway? It may be in catching a vision of the value of the end product to people.

Whenever I board an airplane, for example, I hope very much that the mechanics have seen the value of what they do and have performed the work accordingly! I hope they have not let musing about the meaning of life in general take the place of being careful to do their job down to the last detail in particular. My safety depends on it.

People sometimes have a hard time looking all the way to the end user of the results of their work. In that case, they may find the value of such work by looking to the next workstation that depends on the work and employing their skills in the best manner so that the workstation can add value to the product also. This is one of the key techniques of total quality management.

Meaning certainly will be found also in developing and using one's skills in human relationships to show care toward fellow workers. As Anne Rowthorn, a layperson who seeks to encourage other laypersons to see their work as ministry, wrote:

> However routine most work may be, human relationships on any job are never routine. . . . The respect, consideration, care, even sympathy with which we approach our fellow workers is important . . . . By our being, through our being, we serve Christ in our fellow workers.[8]

Use Your Unique Skills in Your Work

As one approaches the choice of a job, an important question to ask is this: Does this job involve enough of the true me for me to give a significant portion of my life to it—at least my life for the foreseeable future, until I can find a job more compatible with who I am?

Most jobs call for trade-offs about aspects of the job that are more attractive and less attractive, more satisfying and less satisfying, more meaningful and less meaningful. People, including people of faith, rarely find perfect jobs. Some jobs are so incompatible with our unique skills and gifts, we would do well to take action at the first opportunity either to restructure the job so that it does fit us or to find a job that is more compatible.

Harvard professor Shosanna Zuboff interviewed many workers about how they felt about their work, particularly about how they were dealing with changes brought about by technology. One worker displayed keen insight when he said, "If you don't let people grow and develop and make decisions, it's a waste of human life—a waste of human potential. If you don't use your knowledge and skill, it's a waste of life."[9]

We might go further and paraphrase the last sentence as follows: If you don't find ways to use your knowledge and skills—your gifts as a person of faith—on the job, it's a waste of these gifts.[10] To the extent that you fail to employ them or fail to recognize the basic spiritual nature of these gifts, you likely are missing the meaning in your work that God intends and that you could and should be experiencing.

Seek to Create Beauty
and Order Through Your Work

The idea of work as divine assignment is rooted in God's command to humankind to "fill the earth and subdue it; and have dominion over the fish of the sea and over the birds of the air and over every living thing that moves upon the earth" (Gen 1:28). The command is in harmony with God's work of bringing order, light, and beauty out of chaos, darkness, and emptiness.

Some work and the product of that work have more potential for order and beauty in them than others, certainly. Still, almost every job comes with a certain degree of chaos and thus a certain degree of potential for developing order and beauty. Our work as human beings and as people of faith has to do with bringing order and beauty out of whatever amount of chaos exists. This is as much so in the world of work as in every other part of our world.

When we are using our unique gifts to do work that helps others, we simultaneously have the opportunity to carry out our divine assignment. The result, especially when we have evidence that we've done our jobs well, can be a sense of intrinsic meaning in our work and in the products we've created.

A computer operator may have this feeling of meaning when she's been able to work out a particular piece of code successfully. An automobile mechanic may sense this intrinsic meaning in his work when he's been able to locate the mysterious source of a car's problem and fix it. A business leader may feel it when she's been able to lead a company to produce a useful product that provides a profit for her company and thus enables workers to remain employed and participate in the company's success.

Because the experience of this sort of intrinsic meaning in our work is in line with the biblical view of work, we would do well to consider such moments carefully and see them as more than human occasions. We should see that they are spiritual in nature, and we should revel in the meaning we find in them.

Meaning in an Epitaph

An epitaph on a tombstone is said to read, "Here lies the body of Thomas Jones, born a man, died a grocer." Substitute any occupation you wish for "grocer," and the result is the same for Thomas Jones, or any of us. The epitaph suggests that Mr. Jones somehow stopped being a human being, made in God's image, and became only a person engaged in a given occupation.

It's easy to get trapped or enticed into living in that manner. We can too easily become corporate men and women, focused only on our occupations within the world of work. When we do, we ignore or relegate to positions of little importance the human and spiritual facets of our lives.

Contrast Thomas Jones's epitaph with another's. An epitaph on one Thomas Cobb's ancient tombstone is said to read like this:

> To Thomas Cobb
> Who mended shoes
> In this village
> For forty years
> TO THE GLORY OF GOD.

Thomas Cobb evidently used his unique skill in his seemingly mundane work of helping people wear well-fitting shoes. Perhaps in addition to the shoes being his way of helping others, they also were objects of beauty to him, into which he had poured his unique gifts. If even only part of this speculation concerning Thomas Cobb's life be true, he's not a bad model for the rest of us who seek meaning in our work. Beyond our speculation, the epitaph indicates that evidently those who observed his work saw in it more than simply the act of stitching and nailing leather together; they saw that the cobbler's work was for the glory of God. That's the ultimate meaning to be poured into and out of our work, however mundane it may appear.

Perhaps it is as theologian Matthew Fox wrote: "If all things come from God, then even work has God as its source. Perhaps especially our work comes from God."[11] At least work has that potential in our lives. It is up to us to actualize that potential through our choice of work and our approach to that work.

Notes

[1]Stephen R. Covey, *Principle-Centered Leadership* (New York: Simon & Schuster, 1991) 291.

[2]Ernst Friedrich Schumacher, *Good Work* (New York: Harper & Row, 1979) 27.

[3]G. Agrell, *Work, Toil, and Sustenance* (Verbum: Hakan Ohlssons, 1976) 129, cited with disagreement in Andrew T. Lincoln, *Ephesians,* Word Biblical Commentary (Dallas TX: Word Books, 1990) 42:304.

[4]Robert K. Greenleaf, *Servant Leadership: A Journey into the Nature of Legitimate Power and Greatness* (New York: Paulist Press, 1977) 49, italics in original.

[5]Ibid., 227, italics in original.

[6]Elton Trueblood, *Your Other Vocation* (New York: Harper & Brothers, 1952) 72-73.

[7]Shoshana Zuboff, *In the Age of the Smart Machine: The Future of Work and Power* (New York: Basic Books, 1988) 98.

[8]Anne Rowthorn, *The Liberation of the Laity* (Wilton CT: Morehouse-Barlow, 1986) 88-89.

[9]Zuboff, 414.

[10]See chapter 3, "Can Faith Really Be Lived at Work?" for further discussion of the theme of the use of one's Christian gifts at work, not just on the church property, at church events, or with one's fellow church members.

[11]Matthew Fox, *The Reinvention of Work: A New Vision of Livelihood for Our Time* (San Francisco: HarperSanFrancisco, 1994) 102.

Chapter 7
Relate to Fellow Workers as a Person of Faith

John Cowan, a management consultant, was visiting a factory in a rural area to make suggestions about how to do things better, faster, and cheaper. He noted that the sewing machines the women workers used were all facing one another. He suggested to the plant manager that efficiency could be increased if the machines were repositioned so that they faced away from one another. In that way, the sewing machine operators would not be distracted from their work.

The plant manager agreed that the consultant's suggested arrangement might be more efficient. Then he countered,

> These women are remarkable workers. Our rural production shops outperform the ones in the city. But these women don't come here to work. They come here to talk. They don't need the check that bad. Most of them are farm wives. There is work on the farm, just nobody to talk to. I line these machines up so they can't talk, and they will quit. It wouldn't be fun anymore.[1]

The plant manager was wise enough to recognize the value of human relationships in the world of work. Human beings are made for relationship; the most cleverly designed work processes cannot substitute for attention to this human need.

The current emphasis in business on building teams, developing trust, and encouraging clear and accurate communication among workers recognizes the importance of positive human relationships in the world of work. This emphasis is welcome, as any concern for humanizing the workplace should be. It fits hand-in-glove with faith's concern for encouraging relationships of love and care. Indeed, people who truly practice their faith by putting love and care into their relationships have the opportunity to make a great difference in the arena of work in general and in the lives of individual coworkers in particular.

This chapter suggests specific ways you can relate to your fellow workers as a person of faith who puts into practice the most important tenet of faith—love. If you will implement them in your life at your place of work . . .

- You will aid in setting the tone for the workplace as a whole.
- You may well be able to encourage positive relationships between individual workers where negative or no relationships had existed.
- You may become known as a person who treats other people with fairness and indeed with loving concern.
- You will truly live your faith.
- You may even have opportunities to help others understand the importance and relevance of faith and become people of faith themselves.

Sound like a good deal? So how can you relate to your coworkers as a person of faith?

Make Relating as a Human Being Your Highest Priority

At work as elsewhere, people sometimes forget that they and their coworkers are first of all not job titles, boxes on the corporate organization chart, rungs on the corporate ladder, or even achievers of goals for themselves and the company. Rather, they are first of all human beings. In fact, that's the best they, and any of us, will ever be.

A management group had gone away for a meeting at a retreat setting more than a hundred miles away from the company's headquarters. The location was somewhat inaccessible. A new executive who had been on the job for only a few days was present. Just as the meeting began, the new person received a message from his wife. She had become quite ill, so ill that she was unable to care for their children. Since the family was new to the area as well as to the company, she knew no one who could help. Could he come home?

How would the other members of the management team respond? Would they accept the very human need of the new executive? Would they feel that he was not dependable, that he was not as committed as they thought he was when they hired him, that he did not put the needs of the company first, and that they had made a wrong choice? After all, the new guy obviously was concerned about his wife and family and felt the need to do something to help them in spite of his new job's demands.

The group responded magnificently. One fellow executive called his wife to see whether she could go to the new employee's home and assist his family. She did. Another gave the new executive the name and phone number of the family doctor. A third loaned him a car to make the trip back home. A fourth marked the map to help him find his way.

Is it any accident that the company gets high marks from its customers for the service the company provides?[2] Customer satisfaction begins with the quality of human relationships inside the company.

If you work with and for people who relate in this manner to fellow employees who are in need, you are fortunate. If you relate in this manner to fellow employees who are in need, your fellow employees are fortunate. Furthermore, they likely see you as a person truly living out faith at work.

It's too easy, though, for decision makers, or even fellow employees, to treat the people with whom they work as only employees with skills rather than as human beings with a full life beyond the application of skills on the job. This sort of behavior downgrades people, of course. It occurs when people forget they are human beings first of all, and not employees or managers.

Even people of faith can surrender to the business culture that suggests people are important only for what they can do for the company, not for who they are. Responding to the challenge to live faith at work calls for relating as a human being to one's fellow human beings at work. No amount of religious talk can substitute for this way of behaving and relating.

Rabbi Harold Kushner tells how his teacher Abraham Joshua Heschel used to say that when he was young, he admired clever people; but now that he had become old, he admired kind people. Wisdom leads to valuing kindness at work, too. Clever people are needed in the world of work, no doubt, but they are more helpful if they are also kind, relating to their coworkers as human beings, not merely as walking job titles and sets of skills.[3]

Value Each Person at Work

Relating to other people at work means relating to *all* other people at work. How can Christians justify practicing race, gender, or class discrimination at work any more than they can justify discrimination of any sort anywhere?

The Letter of James provides unmistakably clear guidance about relating positively to all people. James 2:9 warns, "If you show partiality, you commit sin and are convicted by the law as transgressors." This verse occurs near the end of a section that warns against elevating the well-to-do person over a common person—actually a rich person over a poor person. It's true that the setting pictured is a service of worship, but denying the application of the passage to other human relationships, including relationships at work, would be a poor way to interpret the biblical message.

Each of your fellow employees, whether she be CEO or janitor, deserves to be treated with dignity, respect, care, and, in short, love, as much as any other. Most of us know more than a few climbers who speak only to their peers and those above them but not to those below them in the organizational structure if they are not their direct reports—unless they need a favor. What a tragedy, so annoying in the short term and so destructive in the long term. Such behavior is inexcusable for a Christian and is harmful to the cause of Christ.

Human beings at every level in the organization need to be valued and responded to for who they are, whatever their job title, race, gender, religion, or other condition of life. Please do not assume, however, that engaging in such a pattern of relationship is going to be easy, especially if you do it openly and consistently. Jesus himself got into trouble with the authorities because he insisted on treating the outcast with respect, even love, rather than ingratiate himself with the authorities who treated the outcast as an outcast. He associated with sinful people, people who could not meet the standards of the upwardly mobile or the already there. People who aspire to be his followers are expected to follow his example—even at work.

Of course, legal protection is extended today to potential victims of race and gender discrimination in the workplace. Obviously, no Christian should knowingly be involved in such misbehavior. In addition, however, the person of faith who values every person will actively promote positive treatment of every person, rather than merely look for ways to avoid negative treatment. People of faith must be concerned with legal compliance, but with more than mere compliance. They must demonstrate positive relationships with all their fellow human beings at work.

The payoff for the person of faith is the knowledge that he or she is following Jesus' command and example. The payoff for business is the development of a culture that is more effective in bringing health to the company.

How so? Simple. A basic tenet of customer service, the hallmark of business success today, is that employees treat customers the way management treats employees. In fact, this is the most important principle of customer satisfaction; it's indispensable. Employees who perceive they are valued as human beings will value customers as human beings, bringing benefit to the company.[4] Even if your valuing each of your fellow employees somehow is not perceived as a benefit to the company, you have a higher loyalty, don't you?

When you are tempted not to see the value in every person, I suggest you do one thing as a reality check. Remind yourself that every employee you pass in the hall or work beside is probably an expert on something you know nothing about and likely has valuable abilities that may be hidden from you.

Not long ago I attended the funeral of a coworker only a few years older than I. He was a friend, someone who sat at the same lunch table in the cafeteria as I did on occasion. I was surprised at the funeral service to learn of a number of significant and important parts to his life away from work, about which I had no inkling as I worked with him. Interestingly, other coworkers who had known him longer admitted that they, too, learned some things about him at his funeral service they had not known before. He was an accomplished amateur musician, to name one thing.

As I reflected on my discovery of unknown facets of my friend's life, I thought of the facets of my own life of which most of my coworkers would be unaware. As far as I know, I do not purposely keep these facets hidden, but there is no ready opportunity for that sort of self-revelation. The next step in my reflection was to recognize that my fellow workers similarly have hidden areas of their own lives and are likely persons of greater richness than I often recognize.

Help Your Fellow Employees Achieve Their Goals

A friend was in an African country on business. As he prepared to return home, he found he needed to change his airline reservations. In the outlying area where he was staying, all telephone calls from the region went through one person, the town telephone operator.

Unknown to my friend, the telephone operator for the town had quarreled the day before with the telephone operator of the hotel where my friend was staying. My friend got on the telephone, asked the hotel operator to connect him with the town telephone operator, reached the outside operator in the town, and told the person he would like to call the airport in the larger town nearby. The town telephone operator knew that the call was coming from the hotel where he was at odds with the hotel telephone operator. The town telephone operator told my friend that the call could not go through because he was not permitting any calls to be made.

"Oh," my friend asked, "when do you think I can get the call through?"

"Tomorrow," the operator replied.

"But I need to call today," my friend insisted.

"Tomorrow," the operator said.

"Tomorrow?" my friend asked incredulously.

"Tomorrow," the operator insisted firmly.

"I'll call the American embassy," my friend shouted angrily—and with little display of intelligence, he later realized.

"No, you won't," the operator replied.

The next sound my friend heard was the click of a phone being hung up, and that was the end of that for that day.

The following day, my friend rang up the town telephone operator and asked for the airport. The operator replied, with no hint of remembrance of the previous day's conflict, "Why certainly, sir."

Of course, this would never happen in our country, would it? The fact is, poor human relationships likely scuttle many more business activities than any other cause.

People of faith are human beings, too, and they sometimes get caught up in petty—or major—squabbles and acts of rivalry and jealousy. This happens at church, at home, in recreational activities, and even in driving our cars. Why should we not expect it to happen at work as well? The fact is, of course, such behavior is no more right or tolerable at work than it is in any of these other places.

Relating positively to our fellow workers calls for looking for ways to assist, not impede, their work. Indeed, a current business emphasis is that each worker needs to see the next worker downstream in the workflow as her customer. The result of such an approach is that each worker is responsible for doing quality work in order to enable the next worker to perform in a quality manner, too. The ultimate goal, of course, is that their work as individuals, when added together, will produce a quality product and service for the ultimate customer—the outside customer.

This way of relating to coworkers makes sense as a business emphasis, and it makes even more sense for people of faith to seek to be of help at work to their coworkers rather than either ignore or impede their work. Both business productivity and positive human relationships are at stake.

Be Sensitive to Opportunities to Minister to Coworkers

You can be sure that all the people with whom you have contact at work have needs from time to time that they find almost unbearable. They may be confused about their lives; troubled about some personal problem; worried about a child, a parent, or other loved one; concerned about their own physical illness or a family member's; or grieved by the loss of a loved one. The list is as endless and varied as human beings.

Many of your coworkers who face such problems have few other people to whom they can turn for help. Even if they do, they may feel that no one at work understands or cares. But you can be the person whom they know does care.

What can you do? The most important thing may be to listen. Of course, such listening does not mean conducting an in-depth counseling session, even if you were capable of doing such, on company time. In the normal round of human conversation at work, however, most of us have opportunities to ask how things are going and to wait for an answer.

Tom Chappell comments, "I've learned over and over that the best and easiest way for a boss to show his respect for his workers is to listen to them."[5] For management, such listening includes not only workers' personal concerns, but also workers' ideas on how best to do the work itself.

The second most important thing you can do is to use appropriately the information shared. Some information can be talked about with others, and some should be treated as thoughts entrusted to a friend, to be guarded and not shared.

The third thing you can do is to take appropriate action. A responsive word of support may be all that is needed in some cases. A note may help. Sharing in gifts meant to provide comfort at times of illness and loss or to celebrate events of joy may be appropriate in other cases. Giving advice, directing to other people who can help, and providing other resources can also be a part of ministry.

For many people of faith, the workplace is the setting for their greatest opportunities for ministry. These opportunities include ministry through the work itself, but it also includes relating with care and concern for coworkers. Could it be that these natural, immediate opportunities for showing care and concern to people they see every day are the ones people of faith neglect most and most often? The workplace, as every other place, provides a setting where we may encounter Christ in people who have needs (see Matt 25:31-46).

On the lighter side, Philip Crosby, the total quality management guru, observes that people never become so cynical or jaded that they don't consider their birthday to be a special time.[6] Even so simple a thing as remembering a birthday can be an opportunity for ministry. Ministry occurs in the small things as well as in the big things.

If You Are in Management,
Take Special Care in Relating to People

When King Solomon of ancient Israel died, his son Rehoboam suc-
ceeded him. The nation found itself on shaky ground. Would the nation
remain united and possibly continue the golden age enjoyed under
Solomon's leadership?

The accomplishments of Solomon's reign had not come easy.
Everybody didn't like Solomon, to put it bluntly, though they likely
would not have said it to his face while he was alive. The people had
worked hard and borne heavy burdens to support Solomon's building
projects. On behalf of the people, a rival of Rehoboam's asked for
some relief.

King Rehoboam asked for time to think about the request. During
that time, he consulted with the older leaders of the nation; they had
served Solomon while he was alive. The older leaders advised
Rehoboam, "If you will be kind to this people and please them, and
speak good words to them, then they will be your servants forever"
(2 Chron 10:7).

These words provide helpful guidance for any manager of any era.
Alas, Rehoboam rejected this good advice and went with the harsh
approach of the young, driven, would-be management gurus. Rehoboam gave this message to be delivered to the people: "My father
made your yoke heavy, but I will add to it; my father disciplined you
with whips, but I will discipline you with scorpions" (v. 14). As a
result of Rehoboam's insistence on heavy-handed management, the
kingdom split into two, and the portion of the nation over which
Rehoboam presided went down hill.

More recently, management expert Jack Falvey gave advice to
managers in an article in the *Wall Street Journal*. His advice was
similar to the advice Israel's wise elders gave:

> There are no great behavioral science secrets to good management.
> If you will give top priority to supporting and paying your people,
> you will be blessed with results beyond your dreams.[7]

I can illustrate the truth of that advice quite personally and from an
employee's point of view. After weathering the Depression, my father
left the farm to work for a large company. He worked for the company
for more than twenty-five years. He then lived about twenty-five years
longer after he retired. The work my father did was basically manual
labor, and he was decidedly not one of the "big boys" of management,

as he called them. Still, the work and his association with the company meant much to him.

After he retired, Daddy treasured greatly the annual gatherings of retirees the company sponsored for many years. He looked forward to them and never missed one. He kept in a display case all the little gifts the company gave the retirees at these gatherings. One touching act, unforgettable to me as his son, symbolizes unmistakably his loyalty to and appreciation for the company for which he had worked. He gave instructions that at his death he was to be buried in the simple suit the company had given him years earlier. That's what we did when he died not long ago at age eighty-nine.

If you as a manager are ever tempted—like Rehoboam—to try to get results by being hard on your employees, tempted to fail to treat employees as people, tempted to look at the bottom line only and not at the people who can help the company get there, remember Rehoboam. But also, remember my father and all the "little people" like him who are down the ladder from you. You may find it hard to believe, but they probably value the company and their jobs just as much as you do and would work every bit as hard as you to achieve the company's goals—or would if you would get out of the way and permit them to do so. Don't mess things up for them—*and* for the company— by acting like a jerk and calling it "management."

It should be rather obvious that people of faith who are in management have a special responsibility in their relationships with people. They need to listen to and follow the wise advice Rehoboam rejected. Kindness in relating to employees does go further, receive more positive response, and, yes, result in greater productivity than does harshness. As Tom Chappell states, "Any boss who gives people a reason to love going to work is going to see results in productivity that he's going to love."[8]

Management consultant Keki R. Bhote, a leader in developing and implementing productive management techniques, wrote these words that also seem reminiscent of the advice Rehoboam rejected:

> The truly visionary leaders turn the organization upside down . . . .
> They put the customer on top, followed by the front line troops that come into frequent contact with customers. Below them are the support services, followed by middle management. At the bottom of the totem pole is the leader. He becomes a servant—not in a menial sense but in a biblical sense! His role is to serve, to help the doers do their job—by removing roadblocks and providing resources, by becoming a facilitator, a cheerleader, a consultant, a coach, a teacher.

HELP should be the key word at any level of management. A manager that cannot help his people is of little value to the company or his employees.[9]

Max DePree is a person of faith as well as a successful business-man. He advises would-be leaders, "Leadership is a job, not a position. The people who work with you are not your people; you are theirs."[10]

Shouldn't people of faith who are managers follow these sound words of advice that not only achieve practical results in the business world but also are biblically-based? Jesus himself advised,

> You know that among the Gentiles those whom they recognize as their rulers lord it over them, and their great ones are tyrants over them. But it is not so among you; but whoever wishes to be great among you must be your servant, and whoever wishes to be first among you must be slave of all. (Mark 10:42-44)[11]

Share Your Faith in Appropriate Ways

Let me say it clearly and directly. If you are going to act like a jerk or a crook at work, do God and me a couple of favors. First, don't "wit-ness" to anybody else about how to become a Christian. Second, don't even tell anybody you *are* a Christian. Believe me, if you don't tell anybody, no one, but no one, would ever guess it anyway.

Let me stick the point in a little further. (People like that seem to have a hard time getting the point when it's about them.) If you insist on acting like a jerk at the same time you are claiming to be a person of faith and even telling others how to become one themselves, you will do much more harm than good. Either people will know you're a hypocrite, or they'll think that what you are is what Christianity is and reject it. Frankly, I wouldn't blame them either way.

I contend that you will not be able to share your faith verbally in an effective manner until you have become the kind of person depicted by the previous suggestions in this book. The downfall of many peo-ple's attempts to tell others at work about what their faith means to them is right here. These attempts appear to the listeners to be manip-ulative tactics for selling an inferior product for which they have no use and that does not relate to their lives. Why? Because the would-be "witness" has never given attention to demonstrating the truth of the gospel in relating to his or her fellow human beings. If people of faith would give more attention to how they relate to their coworkers, they might well have more and greater opportunities actually to talk about their faith in a natural, positive, helpful manner.

Those who live out their faith at work but say nothing about it will do considerably more good for the cause of faith than those who insist on telling their coworkers about it but at the same time fail to be either good employees or persons who live their faith. Thankfully, these choices are not the only ones available, however. The ideal is to live your faith and also to find appropriate ways of sharing it.

There are good and not-so-good, appropriate and inappropriate, ways of sharing one's faith, of course. Imagine if an airline pilot decided to share his faith with the passengers as the airplane headed into a severe thunderstorm on its final approach to the terminal. Lightning is flashing on every side in an otherwise pitch-dark sky; the plane drops ten thousand feet at a time, like an elevator whose cable has snapped; the flight attendants have been ordered to sit down *now;* and the pilot asks over the intercom, "Are all of you ready to die?" (Having been on more than one such airplane flight in a severe thunderstorm, I can testify that the question would be superfluous anyway. Most passengers would already be asking themselves that question and saying their prayers at that very moment!)

Some of the ways in which well-meaning but shortsighted people of faith attempt to "stand up for their beliefs" at work are as shockingly inappropriate as that. Any action that could be described as harassment, even if it involves religion and even if the person of faith means well, is self-defeating as well as disgusting. Actions that separate employees into those who are people of faith and those who are not—or who are not of my particular faith—and that result in discrimination are intolerable in the workplace, as everywhere else.

Then what is appropriate? The actions of the apostle Paul at work provide guidance.

Paul is portrayed as a tentmaker in Corinth (Acts 18:3), Ephesus (Eph 20:34), and Thessalonica (1 Thess 2:9). When Paul is described as a tentmaker, most often it is assumed that he was a tentmaker in order to support his preaching financially. That assumption would be true, of course, but there may be more to it. In addition to being a tentmaker in order to support his preaching, he may also have shared his faith *while* he worked.[12]

Two lines of evidence support this conclusion. One, the culture of Paul's day recognized the workshop as a place of intellectual, philosophical discussion. Beginning with Socrates, the Greek philosophers had utilized the place of work in that manner. A great leap of logic is not required in order to believe that Paul would have approached the workplace setting as a great opportunity for continuing that tradition and proclaiming the message of the gospel.

Perhaps gathered around Paul as he worked would have been his fellow workers and a few visitors who wanted to know more about the new teaching Paul both taught and lived. As Paul worked with his hands, perhaps he thus also used the opportunity to talk about his faith, just as the secular philosophers had used the workplace as a setting for sharing their ideas.

A second line of evidence for Paul's using the workplace to share his faith is in the Greek text of 1 Thessalonians 2:9. The meaning of the text may include the idea that Paul was "night and day working in order not to burden financially" the Thessalonians and that at the same time he was proclaiming to the Thessalonians the gospel of God. The acts of working and proclaiming would have been simultaneous. Paul proclaimed while he worked.

What does Paul's practice teach us about sharing our own faith at work? First, he did it. Second, he did it in line with accepted social and cultural patterns of his day. Thus, people of faith have the responsibility for sharing their faith at work, and they are also responsible for doing so in ways that are appropriate in the culture of the particular workplace of which they are a part.

My friend and former pastor Ray Vickrey of Dallas suggests that one application of the message of Pentecost in Acts 2 is that people of faith need to let themselves be empowered by the Spirit to speak the message of faith in the language of their culture—which includes their culture as it is found in the workplace.

For some employees, participating in prayer and Bible study sessions at work is an option permitted by their company. These events, handled wisely so that they do not become exclusive cliques, can be helpful opportunities for sharing one's faith.

Whatever your own situation at work, if you will first become known as a person who is trustworthy and competent as an employee, who works for the good of the company and demonstrates care for every coworker regardless of the person's level in the company hierarchy, you will not lack for opportunities to share your faith in natural, appropriate ways at work. This often means simply adding to one's behavioral witness the verbal witness of telling others what your faith means to you and how it came to have a place in your life.

For a great many people of faith at work, the place to begin is not in talking but in living. The talk can then flow out of the living. This sequence is both more natural and authentic than feeling one must find the right words to say to sell one's faith to someone else.

Hell, Heaven, or Someplace in Between?

Which idea best describes your own work setting—hell, heaven, or someplace in between? My hunch is, heaven it's not; it's certainly not for most workers. Even so, you have the opportunity to make your workplace more like heaven, a place where God's will is done on earth as it is in heaven.

A key element in making this change has to do with human relationships. The kind of workplace that is more like heaven on earth is a place where people relate to one another as human beings, where all people are valued, where people work together instead of in competition with one another, where people show care—love—for each other by helping one another with their human needs as well as with their work, and where employees and management treat each other with respect.

If you will work toward this kind of workplace, you will do yourself and your fellow human beings a world of good. You will enhance, rather than detract from, the opportunities for spreading the good news of God's love. This is not only good religion; it supports rather than conflicts with the goals of good business.[13]

Notes

[1]John Cowan, *Small Decencies: Reflections and Meditations on Being Human at Work* (New York: HarperBusiness, 1992) 62.

[2]Ibid., 67.

[3]Harold Kushner, *When All You've Ever Wanted Isn't Enough* (New York: Pocket Books, 1986) 58.

[4]See Joan Koob Cannie with Donald Caplan, *Keeping Customers for Life* (New York: AMACOM, 1991) 148; see also Thomas K. Connellan and Ron Zemke, *Sustaining Knock-Your-Socks-Off Service* (New York: AMACOM, 1993) 150.

[5]Tom Chappell, *The Soul of a Business: Managing for Profit and the Common Good* (New York: Bantam Books, 1993) 68.

[6]Philip B. Crosby, *Running Things: The Art of Making Things Happen* (New York: New American Library, 1986) 236.

[7]Jack Falvey, "To Raise Productivity, Try Saying Thank You," David Asman and Adam Meyerson, eds., *The Wall Street Journal on Management: The Best of the Manager's Journal* (New York: New American Library, 1985) 79.

[8]Chappell, 69.

[9]Keki R. Bhote, *Next Operation as Customer (NOAC): How to Improve Quality, Cost, and Cycle Time in Service Operations* (New York: American Management Association, 1991) 104.

[10]Max DePree, *Leadership Jazz* (New York: Dell Publishing, 1992) 169-70.

[11]See also Ephesians 6:9, which deals with the relationship of master and slave, but which is very clear that Christian masters are to avoid harsh treatment of their slaves. If such instruction was appropriate for the relationship of master and slave, it is certainly applicable to the relationship of manager and employee.

[12]Ronald F. Hock, "The Workshop as a Social Setting for Paul's Missionary Preaching," *Catholic Biblical Quarterly,* 41 (July 1979):438-50. See also John B. Polhill, *Acts,* The New American Commentary, vol. 26 (Nashville TN: Broadman Press, 1992) 384, citing that article.

[13]For additional guidance in building positive relationships at work, see my previous book, *How to Be Happier in the Job You Sometimes Can't Stand* (Nashville TN: Broadman Press, 1990) chapter 4, "Build Positive Relationships," and chapter 5, "Handle Criticism Carefully."

Chapter 8
Choose How You Balance Life

Psssst. Want a balanced life, a life without rushing, a life where you are able to spend the time necessary to take care of all the important things, a life where you feel in control? You do? What will you give for it?

If having such a life were as simple as exchanging a few dollars for some sure-fire, long-lasting relief from the rush of life, most Americans would make the deal in a moment. But how elusive it is to achieve such a goal. We can verify this thought quite easily. Just observe the pushiness, even anger, displayed in traffic on the way home from work as people jockey for a better position to get themselves home or to the daycare center more quickly.

A young mother, face drawn taut like a race car driver's, whizzes by me in her car, quickly leaving me far behind. She's traveling at least fifteen miles over the speed limit. The infant car seat is empty. The car weaves in and out of traffic as the sun goes down.

A middle-aged driver cruises past the line of merging cars and then, at the head of the line, niftily manipulates his bumper ahead of the first car. As he does, I note the radar detector on his dash and the telltale sign of the fish on the trunk of his car. The fish evidently signifies that he—or someone in the family—thinks of himself as a faithful Christian. Or could the car belong to his wife?

If you live in a small town where two cars waiting at the traffic light constitute a traffic jam, you may not have experienced the wonder of trying to balance life as a person of faith at the same time you spend an hour or more in your car on the way to and from your eight- to ten-hour day at work, after which the kids have ball practice, Scouts, band and/or choir; and both you and your spouse, who drives in the exact opposite direction to another job, have committee meetings at church; plus when you take a moment to listen to your telephone answering machine, you hear the concerned voice of your mother saying your father is in the hospital 200 miles away and may undergo surgery the day after tomorrow. I'll bet you've experienced a part of this, though, and probably more.

You perhaps wouldn't be surprised, then, to know that in a recent survey, 38% of Americans said they "always felt rushed." This percentage is up from 32% in 1985 and 22% in 1971. Look at those who feel the most time pressure: (1) they are ages 25-54; (2) they work full time; (3) they are parents. How many of those categories do you fit in? Furthermore, more women than men feel this sense of being rushed, but the difference is not great—37% of the women as compared to 33% of the men.

The percentage of a category feeling they are rushed jumps to 64% of mothers who have jobs outside the home and 72% of single mothers who work. A brilliant television commercial describes a product as being "for mothers who have a lot of love but not a lot of time." The people who thought that slogan up are tuned in to a prime concern of working mothers today.

Indeed, most people, whatever their particular role in life, would have a similar concern. Life is just whirling by too fast. We may feel we are doing some important, worthwhile things, but we also feel we're having to neglect too many other important, worthwhile things at the same time. Moreover, this feeling of being rushed is growing stronger. Almost half (48%) of the survey participants said they had less leisure time than they did five years ago.[1]

What's the Rush?

Where does this feeling of being rushed come from, the feeling that life is out of balance and bumping about like an overloaded washing machine? It stems from at least six sources. Maybe you can think of even more.

We want money.

First, money for individuals and their families drives people to work long hours. Researcher and author Juliet Schor recently observed that we could work half as much as we do right now if we would content ourselves with the standard of living that existed in 1948. Schor says, "We could now produce our 1948 standard of living (measured in terms of marketed goods and services) in less than half the time it took in that year."[2] How so? In the first two decades after 1948, productivity increased at 3% each of those years. Since those two decades, the increase in productivity each year has been smaller, averaging just slightly more than 1% a year. Still, the arithmetic indicates how greatly total productivity has increased since 1948.

What did Americans choose to do with this increase in productivity? They did not choose to reduce their work hours. Then what did they use it for? They used it to buy more things—so they would be required to continue to work to pay for these things and to buy more of them. Schor comments, "In 1990, the average American owns and consumes more than twice as much as he or she did in 1948, but also has less free time."[3]

How did you or most people you know live in 1948? I was but a child at the time (really), but I know from intense and vivid personal experience that my family didn't have indoor plumbing. We had no television either. We did have a radio and a scratchy Victrola (that's an antiquated record player to you young folks) on which I recall listening to Gene Autry sing, "Here Comes Santa Claus." We did not have central heating and air conditioning. In 1948, electricity and a telephone had only recently reached my family's home. We did not have a new car. Our well-used car had neither air conditioning nor an automatic transmission, and I did not know of anyone who had a car with those conveniences—not even the town doctor. I'm writing these lines on a computer, but obviously no one had a home computer in those days. No one in my family had gone to college; I did not know personally anyone who had.

Although some people in the United States undoubtedly enjoyed such things my family lived without in 1948, these modern conveniences had not become so widely dispersed that people took them for granted, as most people do now. At least they hadn't told my family where and how to get them!

Would you want to return to the good old days of 1948? Would I? In the words I recall hearing from my grandfather Peevy, "People ask me about going back to the good old days. I don't want the good old days. I remember how they were!"

And so we continue to rush. Why? To get money to buy things and to pay for the things we've already bought, of course. We buy new and wonderful things that have come along much more recently than 1948—CD players, large-screen televisions, riding lawn mowers, two or even three cars with power windows, and trips to the Caribbean or Hawaii. Oh, it's not that we really want these things for ourselves, you understand, but our children need and want these things.

We have even increased our rushing in order to get these things. Schor's studies indicate that it doesn't just seem as if we are working more hours; we *are* working more hours. From 1969 to 1987, the time the average employed person put in at work increased by 163 hours annually.

Think what this increase means in practical terms. This total indicates an increase of an extra month of work per year, almost an extra half-day of work per week, almost an extra hour of work per day.[4]

Maybe that doesn't seem like much, but how many extra straws are required to break an overloaded camel's back, and how many extra pieces of laundry in a washing machine are required to get it out of balance?

Our desire for things is a part of the reason for this increase in work hours. Some people deliberately work longer hours on their job. Also, moonlighting—working more than one job—is now higher than at any time in the three decades for which records exist.[5] The next reason, "Business wants money," also relates directly to this particular reason and affects profoundly the lives of many employees today who fear they will lose their jobs in the next cutback.

Business wants money.

Since the early 1980s, businesses have generally increased the amount of work time required of the existing workforce rather than hire new workers.[6] Hiring additional workers is more costly than requiring additional work of existing workers.

Adding employees is especially costly in at least two major ways. For one thing, simply requiring additional work of the existing workforce avoids the extra outlay for each new employee's benefits. In addition, by requiring extra work from existing employees, business must expend less effort and expense to ramp up when business is good and to decrease labor resources if business falls off.

This approach by business leads to fear on the part of many employees. These employees fear they will lose their jobs in the next cutback if they don't demonstrate their worth and loyalty to the company. They believe that working the longer hours is necessary to protect themselves. So employees work the longer hours not only because they want things (greed?), but because they don't want to run the risk of losing their jobs (fear, definitely).

Society has expanded the options and raised its expectations.

Society has expanded the options and raised its expectations. You may agree readily with the first part of this statement. After all, the increase in the availability of options of things to have and places to go—both good and not-so-good—is rather self-evident. But has society raised its expectations? Really? How?

A couple of illustrations: First, I formerly lived in a metropolitan area that covered many, many miles. From one side of the metroplex known as Dallas/Fort Worth to the other was seventy-five miles or so. If my wife and I were invited to an event in a part of the metroplex different from the part in which we lived, it would have sounded to lots of people like a flimsy excuse to say, "We can't come. It's just too far." After all, it was expected that one have a car capable of traveling the distance, and freeways connected the most far-flung areas of the metroplex.

In reality, depending on whether the traffic was horrible or merely awful, one could spend a couple of hours getting from Point A to Point B in our hometown, though. A distance that would have been considered a major trek for which one would have made elaborate plans (change the oil; pack a lunch) in an earlier day became simply the done, expected thing. Society had expanded the options and raised its expectations.

Second, whereas in earlier days a high school degree and then later a college degree were considered the door-openers to a life of almost-guaranteed attainment and success, such is no longer the case. The post-graduate degree and even a doctor's degree now are required to generate a similar level of approval (unless one can run lightning-fast, hit people really hard, or put a ball or a puck in a goal an incredible percentage of the time).

Society has expanded the options and raised the expectations in other ways, too. Take housework, for instance. In spite of the invention of numerous labor-saving devices, the amount of time spent on housework (by housewives almost exclusively, of course) has been relatively constant through all this century. Various studies through the years have revealed these figures for the number of hours spent per week on housework: 56 hours per week in 1914; 52 hours per week in 1927 and again in 1929, 1936, 1943, and 1953; 56 hours per work in 1967-68; and 53 hours per week in 1973. Amazingly consistent, isn't it?

Why, you and I may—and should—ask, haven't technology's labor-saving devices really provided better living electrically and reduced the amount of time required for housework? After all, aren't they called *labor-* and *time*-savers? In some cases, technology has indeed helped. In other cases, labor saved in one area has merely been shifted to another. Having a refrigerator, for example, eliminated the need for daily shopping in some cases. But since the local grocery with door-to-door delivery found its business hurt when day-to-day shopping diminished, the supermarket arose, generally with greater travel time required to get to and from the supermarket.

In other cases, society's standards simply rose along with the technology. When automatic washers and dryers were introduced for the home, for example, they did decrease the time needed for washing and drying clothes. Guess what, though. The amount of time spent laundering clothes went up, not down.

Why? More loads of clothes were done at home. First, some clothes now being laundered at home were formerly sent out to commercial laundries. The result was more, not less, laundry time required at home. Second, we developed higher standards of cleanliness. After all, how could we justify wearing clothes that were even slightly soiled now that everyone knew we had a washing machine?[7] Society had expanded the options and raised its expectations.

Having more options available is great. Having higher expectations may be quite okay also. Nevertheless, the expanded options and higher expectations may require more time, not less, and thus contribute to our lives getting out of balance. Keeping up with the Joneses' requires ever greater outlays of time and effort because the Joneses' just can't be satisfied and keep raising the standards.

We have not responded appropriately to the increased percentage of women who work outside the home.

In 1966, slightly more than 40% of women worked in the laborforce outside the home. In 1994, this figure had jumped to slightly more than 60%. The rate of increase indicated by these United States Department of Labor statistics represents a revolution with which society in general, men in particular, and likely even women themselves have not come to terms. This change in women's participation in the laborforce outside the home—and the failure to respond appropriately to it—contributes to the feeling of time pressure, the sense that life is out of balance.

Women, in fact, likely have been thwarted the most in their quest for a life of balance. Society has required an impossible balancing act of them. The problem starts at the most basic level. Consider this: Men generally are affirmed in their work *because* they are good providers for their families. On the other hand, women often find themselves having to prove that they are good wives and mothers *even though* they do work outside the home.[8]

Women with families also find themselves working most, perhaps almost all, of the "second shift" of child care and housework that must be done when parents come home from their jobs.[9] This situation often serves to keep life continually out of balance in two-job households.

Women would obviously and especially feel this pressure, since they actually do most if not all of such work. The pressure also affects men, though. Men who do not do housework at all, not even to mention windows, may find themselves unblissfully ignorant of why housework is somehow expected of them now that their wives are working. On the other hand, men who do perform some household chores and child care have less time to do other things, including nothing, than formerly. The adjustment to women's working outside the home has not been easy and largely has not taken place yet, either in the marital relationship, the workplace, or in other institutions, including the church.

Of course, employers have some responsibility in employees' relating work and home. Companies that want to keep good employees are finding they must help them—*all* of them, women *and* men—balance their work and family commitments appropriately. Such actions are not simply the company's "being good" to its employees; they are also to the company's business advantage. Happy employees are more productive. In addition, if the company has the goal of retaining good employees rather than going through the hassle of replacing them when they leave, then meeting the work/family needs of employees is an important business reason for such actions. Some companies, even with the Family Leave Act of 1993, are more sensitive and helpful in this area than others, of course.

We misuse our time at work, thus spending excessive time there that could be used better elsewhere.

Another source of imbalance in life is that people misuse their time at work, thus spending excessive time there that could be used better elsewhere. This source of imbalance applies mainly to salaried personnel, of course. They tend to have more discretion in how they spend their time at work. People sometimes stay at work for long hours for no good reason other than ego needs, regardless of what other excuse they may actually give. People in management are especially prone to such behavior, although other professionals are also susceptible. How does this happen?

You can probably figure this out by asking yourself this question: Why are people promoted into management? Careful now; I know what you're probably thinking, but I'm serious. Generally, the answer is something like this: People are promoted into management because they are seen to be dedicated to the company and compatible with management above them, of course, but also because they demonstrate special competence in a skill area. (She is an excellent accountant, salesperson, editor, and so on. Let's make her the manager. Besides, none of the rest of her peers are as good as she is.)

Fine and dandy. Aside from the fact that the new manager may or may not have any managerial skills, how will the new manager approach his job? What the new manager does next, after promotion, in his use of time, is crucial. One of the major time-usage temptations of the manager—new or experienced—who has technical competence in the area she supervises is to continue to do some or all of the technical work she does so well and that attracted attention to her in the first place. Or the manager flees to that technical work when he does not know what to do in the management responsibilities. The manager then adds the technical work to the managerial responsibilities.

Technically-competent managers get pulled back—or pull themselves back—into technical work for various reasons. All of the reasons generally are related to ego needs, though. First, people seem to understand better what managers do, or at least give them more respect, when managers describe their identity as an engineer or an accountant, say, than when they describe themselves as managers. Second, they are justifiably proud of their area of technical competence. Third, they already know they are good at their technical specialty, and doing it instead of the more nebulous task of management gives them more immediate, positive feedback.[10]

People other than managers also misuse their time at work to meet ego needs, of course. The desire to impress people with the time one puts in at work can be as powerful a motivator as money. The joy of the chase to accomplish some task can also overshadow the desire for accomplishing balance in all of the areas of one's life. If you find yourself doing these things and can't or won't stop, then be honest with yourself about what is going on rather than rationalizing that you (a) have to do it or (b) are doing it, after all, for the welfare of your family.

People use time poorly at work in other ways, too, including failing to plan, failing to delegate properly, and failing to use peak energy times for peak projects. The list of ways to use time poorly is extensive. The point is, achieving balance calls for attention to how one uses time at work as well as time in other settings of one's life.

Of course, legitimate demands at work or elsewhere require sometimes what appears to be an over-emphasis of time spent in that area. A special project at work may indeed call for extra time, to the apparent neglect of other areas of your life. If the situation is limited in duration and frequency, that's understandable. If the situation is continuous, maybe you need to examine more carefully what's going on and figure out what you need to do to maintain balance more effectively.[11]

We misuse our time away from work.

The features of time include both duration (meaning the number of hours and minutes available) and quality (referring to how effectively we invest those increments of time). The Greek language, in which the New Testament was written, recognized these two features with different words—*chronos,* meaning duration of time, and *kairos,* referring to value and meaning of time.

Effective time usage involves not simply having certain amounts of time available, but also finding ways to leverage that time to achieve your highest goals. Time away from work also needs to be spent well so as to get the most value from it and encourage you to achieve balance in your life.

Most people have their own set of ways in which they misuse time away from work. Maybe it's failing to plan the use of their time. Maybe it's adding item after item of sort-of-good ways to spend their time while neglecting the best.

High on many Americans' list of time-wasters would be television. Business consultant and author Karl Albrecht has applied a colorful image to television. He called it "chewing gum for the mind."[12] What do you look like when you chew gum? Talking? Well, in chewing gum, you move your jaws, but communication is nil. Another image that comes to mind is eating. In chewing gum, you spend a lot of time chewing, but little nourishment results.

Aside from the intellectual malnutrition and miscommunication that occur from a steady diet of watching television, there's an even greater tragedy: the failure to invest the time in activities that are more productive on the one hand or better sources of leisure on the other, whichever one needs at a given moment.

We can indeed have fifty-plus television channels available and there be nothing on, as many of us can attest personally. (But some of us still want to click through all fifty-plus just in case. How could I possibly know that?) Meanwhile, time is passing, and we feel rushed.

Practical Ways to Achieve Balance in the Use of Time

Question: What do you call doing the same thing over and over again but expecting different results each time?
Answer: Insanity.

Unfortunately, according to Einstein's definition, the way we often approach different projects would qualify as insanity. Trying to balance our time would be one such project. Maybe Einstein wasn't so smart after all. Or maybe we're the ones who aren't.

If balancing our lives is a problem, we likely need to step back, take a fresh look, and apply some new approaches. In the hope that you might agree with Einstein, here are some practical steps you can take to make some changes that will enable you to achieve a better sense of balance in your life.

Recognize the need to choose.

Work as fast as you can, as long as you can, in as organized a manner as you can, and you will still have to face this bit of reality: You can't do everything. You may not like to be limited thus, but it's still a fact you must face: You can't do everything. Perhaps you can do more, perhaps you can do more faster, perhaps you can organize better so you can do more faster. Likely you can. You still must fact this fact: You can't do everything.

No human being has been able to do everything. You can't do everything either. In fact, where did you ever get the idea you *could* do everything? Indeed, where did you ever get the idea that doing everything was a good idea? No, not even from God. Nowhere in the Bible did God ever say to anyone, "Stand up, my child, and lift your eyes to the distant horizon. Good. Now, put your nose to the grindstone, and go forward. I want you to do everything." I defy you to find such a Scripture passage.

The fact is you can't do everything. The corollary to this bit of reality is that since we can't do everything, we have to choose what we *will* do. This practical principle is the most important principle of achieving balance in life. Nothing is more important for helping us keep our lives from being scattered and unbalanced than the recognition that we can't do everything—and then going on to build on this important truth.

Dave Thomas tells how he learned this principle for himself. Before he founded Wendy's, he was struggling to establish a successful restaurant and not doing very well at it. In fact, he was about to go broke. His creditor, a fellow named Sanders, Colonel Sanders, felt Thomas was indeed about to go broke. Thomas was trying to do everything in the restaurant and have something for everybody. His menu of offerings was quite lengthy. The number of items on the menu was so great that he had to invest a large amount of money in inventory in order to have available all the ingredients for producing all of the menu items.

One day while Dave was pondering the possibility of going broke, he began to analyze what he was doing. He began to realize he could not do everything in that one restaurant. So, instead of expanding the menu offerings, he decided to cut back and focus on the few important items people seemed to really like.

What happened? Business began to get better. In fact, business got very good. Dave not only survived; he flourished. Dave Thomas realized he had found the answer to his problem and that the answer could apply in all of life. The basic answer is to simplify, to choose, in order to make room for the things that really are important.[13]

Even the biblical characters we admire didn't do everything. In stating how he lived, Paul himself said he did "one thing," not a multiplicity of things: "But this one thing I do" (Phil 3:13). Okay, you may not be able to get it down to "one thing," but you may be able, like Paul, to develop an overarching goal for your life. The point is, you can't do everything; you have to choose. Paul did; so do you.

Once you've convinced yourself of this, an array of approaches is available to help you make the best use of your time and so to balance your life. Further, the irony of recognizing that you are limited and cannot do everything will empower you to focus on accomplishing what is really important.

Determine your unique time-spending opportunities; discard all others.

The previous suggestion calls for developing a fresh perception of ourselves: we can't do everything. Such a perception may be painful, and it may require constant effort on our part to reinforce. The second suggestion is not any easier. In fact, it's even harder.

It takes us into the wider world of our relationships with all sorts of people and groups who feel they have justifiable claims on our time. Many of these people have a rather powerful arsenal at their disposal to persuade us that we should invest this or that chunk of our time in the activities they believe are important. Included in this arsenal may be a personal relationship with us, an economic claim on us, a belief that a cause deserves our sympathy, plus an old standby, the capacity for tapping into feelings of guilt. These people may even suggest that they are certain the activity they have in mind for us is God's will.

In addition, most of us are quite capable of making a request an opportunity to operate from the egocentric position dealt with in the first suggestion. We may activate the notion that "Yes, I can do everything, including this." Whatever the motivation, soon we find our lives out of balance.

What's the answer? We must determine the time-spending opportunities that are uniquely ours and discard those that aren't. How? I suggest you invite all time-spending opportunities to a set of stairsteps to help you discover whether a given way of spending your time is the best way, or even an appropriate way. Make these opportunities climb the steps one by one before you say yes.

Step # 1: Purpose. What exactly would you like to accomplish in your life anyway? Having a purpose in life is a marvelous asset. It's rather like having a destination for a journey. Both a destination for a journey and a purpose for a life enable a person to chart a course in the right direction, channel energies toward getting to the destination, and save time along the way.

Purpose is the chief test to use in distinguishing what truly is important from what merely seems urgent. Successful time-balancing requires us to clarify our highest purposes so we can be better able to follow them.

John Cowan, management consultant and minister, challenges, "Do not allow the daily demands to interfere with seeing the colors of the day or the shadows of the night."[14] Time management experts Merrill and Donna Douglas say it this way: "We should ask ourselves this question: 'If I were to die today, would I be pleased with the way I have spent my time?' "[15] Marian Wright Edelman of the Children's Defense Fund captures the struggle in these words:

> There are so many noises and pulls and competing demands in our lives that many of us never find out who we are. Learn to be quiet enough to hear the sound of the genuine within yourself.[16]

Such expressions reflect what we want, don't they? So how can we get what we want? We first must know what it is, and knowing what it is calls for examining and clarifying our purpose in life.

The Douglasses' suggest this helpful process for identifying specific purposes:

(1) Identify the major areas of your life, perhaps seven or so areas, such as spiritual life, family concerns, career, social life, physical health, mental growth, and financial security. Or you might use the roles you play as the major categories—such as spouse, parent, child, person of faith, employee.

(2) Write one of these as the heading for each of the pieces of paper.
(3) List what you'd like to accomplish in each of these areas during your lifetime.[17]

Next ask yourself these questions:

(1) If I keep on doing what I am doing or accept the particular additional "opportunity" to use my time that is offered, will I be able to do these things?
(2) What do I need to say no to, and what do I need to say yes to in order to achieve my goals?

Step # 2: Ability. Can you actually perform this particular task—well? If not, are you really the right person to do this?

I've discovered through many trials and an equal number of errors that plumbing evidently is a skill I do not have. Almost everything I've tried in this area has resulted in miserable failure, including tons of wasted time. My plumbing scenario has consistently gone like this: (1) Discover problem—or have problem called to my attention. (2) Try to fix problem. (3) Call good plumber.

After each such plumbing experience, I have reflected humbly on the situation, trying to learn what I did wrong and how I could have handled the situation better. I decided that trying to fix the problem was where I went wrong every time. Now I've reduced the solution to plumbing problems from a three-step formula to a two-step formula. Guess which item I omitted. Why did I omit that one? For one thing, it saves a lot of time.

Step # 3: Need. How important is it to do this task? This step is important, but it's the one to which most of us are most susceptible to an emotional appeal, especially guilt. Remember, it's not the only step on the list, though.

The problem is, in many cases wants are often presented to us disguised as needs. How can the extent of the need be determined? Try these tests:

(1) *How far down toward a basic human need is the request?* If the need is as urgent and basic as an infant's cry for food, then it obviously should be considered more important than, say, attending a social function at which someone believes you should be seen. Or, if the need presented will result in the loss of one's job if one doesn't agree to fill it, then most people would say the request ought to have a serious

claim on one's time. But what if fulfilling the work request simply means more money or greater social approval from some person or group of people? Then the request needs to be considered in light of one's other life values.

Unfortunately, employees often face work demands—perhaps choices, perhaps commands—that call for extra outlays of time, with these work demands having little apparent relationship to authentic needs. An organization faced a year-end crush of work every year, necessitating vast amounts of extra work hours. Because most of the employees involved were salaried, the extra work did not bring extra pay. Too, the ordinary work demands were so consistently heavy that "comp time" later on was an unrealistic dream. The work demands simply had to be met.

Unfortunately, too, the extra work resulted from a cause no more worthy than the manner in which the organization kept its financial books. The extra work time did not change the amount of resources the company had, and neither did it change the satisfaction level of its external customers. Work simply had to be completed within the calendar year in order for the expenses to be charged to that calendar year. Someone in the organization was able to get excited about such a goal, but the employees called on for the extra work could find little intrinsic motivation in it.

Still, the company insisted that this goal be met. How should these employees respond? They had little recourse in the matter of *whether* they would comply with the company's work demands. Their only alternative was in *how* they would approach the demand. What did they do? They accepted the absurdity of the situation and worked as a team to complete the work on time. Sometimes that's the only choice when the company makes demands and doesn't plan appropriately either for accomplishing them or explaining them in a clear, positive manner to employees. What can a person of faith do in such a situation? A person of faith caught in such a situation can certainly contribute teamwork and a positive attitude, as positive as possible given the negatives.

(2) *Who has the need or is communicating the need?* Time management expert William Oncken developed a wonderful approach to helping managers manage time.[18] To an extent, all employees can use this approach profitably, and the approach can also be used outside the workplace. Oncken suggested that managers have not one, not two, but three kinds of time. They must learn to manage all of them if they are to be successful at work.

The first kind of time is "boss-imposed time." The activities in boss-imposed time encompass what one does at work because one has a boss who thinks up or passes along things for her subordinates to do. Every worker understands this kind of time. It's unlikely that any employee will be around very long if he or she doesn't!

The second kind of time at work is "system-imposed time." The activities in system-imposed time are what an employee does in order to accomplish the company's goals in cooperation with his peers. System-imposed time is spent performing tasks one needs to do because he is part of an organizational system that requires maintenance and cooperation in order to work—to the extent it works, Oncken observed realistically!

The third kind of time in companies is "self-imposed time." This is so-called discretionary time, which the employee can use to advance the good of the company and himself beyond what is expected. Such time is the time spent doing things one does as a result of personal initiative, creativity, and resourcefulness. The availability of this kind of time probably decreases the farther down the organizational ladder one goes.[19]

Oncken's observations ring true with life in most, if not all, companies. This is somewhat interesting, you may be saying. But you may also be asking what this has to do with living your faith in the world of work. The answer? It comes in two parts.

First, recognizing the givens of business life is as important for the person of faith as it is for every other person. How one manages the time available at work from the various sources—the boss, the system, and one's "own" time—is a measure of stewardship of the time at work and, for salaried personnel, an opportunity for achieving balance in all of life. The challenge is to manage properly all three kinds of time —boss-imposed, system-imposed, and self-imposed. If you can accomplish the work each week in forty-two hours instead of sixty hours, you've just added eighteen hours per week to your time available for achieving a life of balance.

Question: Can people really maintain the appropriate balance in life—work, family, church, friendships, recreation—when they are working sixty hours per week? *Answer:* Few in number are the people who can do that. And, you're not one of them. If you insist on saying you are, don't take your answer for it. Ask your family and friends who are close enough to be brutally honest with you, if you really want the truth.

Second, and more important, in all of life including corporate life, *who* asks us to spend our time in a certain way has significant bearing on *what* we spend our time on. In fact, it needs to. Saying yes or no to many activities calls for consideration of how relationships with significant people in our lives will be affected by the answer we implement. Customers in dire need of our services fit into this category. Those nearest and dearest to us in our families do, too.

Further, we ourselves need and deserve some time for replenishment and growth. Even Jesus did not subject himself to the whims or even the needs of people twenty-four hours a day. He slept when some people thought he should be awake and doing things (Mark 4:38). He deliberately pulled his disciples aside for rest from the pressures of incessant activity (Mark 6:31-32). He went to dinner parties (Matt 9:10; Luke 5:29) and weddings (John 2:1-11). He spent time with children (Matt 19:13-15; Luke 18:15-16). He took time for prayer (Luke 11:1). As busy as he could have been in meeting the demands of the multitude of needy people who tugged at him, Jesus did not give all of his time to such busy-ness.

Step # 4: Availability. If the time-spending opportunity is able to ascend the first three steps, the next question to ask is whether you are available to do the task. Will you have to let go of something else to do this new task?

A scientific law that operates in the natural world states that two objects cannot occupy the same space at the same time. This law applies to events and responsibilities as well as objects. Two events cannot occupy the same time at the same time.

Is the new task really more important than the old task? Will you be able to do justice to both the new task and the old task? Two ways of settling the conflict and determining your availability are to consider the *degree of repetitiveness* of the event and your *role* in the event.

I shudder at writing about degree of repetitiveness. My family has heard me use this idea so much since I learned it years ago as a student of Dr. Wayne Oates, a pioneer in the field of pastoral care. Nevertheless, it's an important guide to availability; it's worked for me numerous times.

Simply stated, here's the principle: Nonrepetitive events take precedence over repetitive ones. For example, wouldn't you agree that attending your child's high school graduation takes precedence over seeing one extra client at work? That particular child won't graduate from high school again. You'll likely have another opportunity to see that client; if not, you'll likely have other clients.

As I'm writing these lines, I'm in a hotel in Atlanta, the hotel that is shaped like a cylinder, a very tall tin can. The time is mid-morning, and I'm writing while my wife is attending a conference at the Georgia World Congress Center. I've opened the curtains so I can see the magnificent view from the forty-ninth floor. It's not the usual thing that I'm here, and neither is it a usual day. It's the Christmas season. In fact, it's the day of the Christmas parade. The streets are blocked off, the crowds are gathering, and excitement is building. I can see marching bands forming and floats lining up.

I tell you, it's beginning to feel a lot like Christmas, and I'm wondering whether I should be watching my computer screen, watching the excitement below, or—perhaps, *perhaps,* perhaps, *perhaps!*— going down to the street so I can actually experience the excitement. I can't even make out the tubas from up here. My being here at parade time is probably close to a nonrepetitive event, my child within me says, so logically. I can write later. What do you suppose I should do? What do you suppose I did? What do you suppose I should have done?

A second guide to availability is *the uniqueness of your role.* I'm my wife's only husband, my son's only father, and my mother's only younger son. In addition, "Granddad" uttered by certain little children has a powerful effect on me. On the other hand, I am—or was—one of many employees in a company, though no one else had the particular responsibility I had.

The nearer my role comes to being unique, the greater the possibility I need to pay attention to the time demands of that role. Sometimes the roles that are farther removed from being unique do need to take precedence for a given period of time, but when the demand of a role that is nearer to being unique is great, someone else will have to perform those other roles.

I can't delegate someone else, for example, to attend a close relative's funeral for me. I may well be able, though, to delegate someone else to teach my Bible study class or work in my place at my place of employment. Perhaps some things that in ordinary circumstances needed to get done just won't get done.

When Joseph Juran, one of corporate America's most noted experts on quality, was eighty-nine years old, an interviewer asked what he would do over again if he were able to do so. His reply? "I know one thing I would do is spend more time with my family."[20] As important as Dr. Juran's work was to corporate America, no one else could fill Dr. Juran's role with his family than Dr. Juran.

Schedule your priorities; don't "prioritize your schedule."

How often have you heard some busy person, perhaps you, say that he or she had to "prioritize my schedule." Prioritizing your schedule is more helpful than doing nothing to manage your time, but prioritizing your schedule doesn't go far enough toward achieving balance in life by managing your time.

Consider: What are you really doing when you're "prioritizing your schedule"? Certainly you're putting the most important items on the list first, following them with items and activities that are successively less important. So what's the problem with that?

The problem is, the raw material you're working with, the activities and demands on your list, may not represent at all the things in your life that you really believe are important. Few of them may relate to *your* purpose in life. If you do every one of those things on your list in order of importance, about the best epitaph that could appear on your tombstone would be this: "The list is finished." In my opinion, "the list is finished" is not exactly what Paul had in mind when he wrote, "I have fought the good fight, I have finished the race, I have kept the faith" (2 Tim 3:7).

Instead of prioritizing your schedule, what should you do? I suggest the following:

(1) *Put the right items on the list you're working from.* These items are the items that actually accomplish the tasks you believe are important. For help in identifying these items, review the activity referred to earlier in this chapter that called for identifying what you'd like to accomplish in the various areas of your life you believe are important.

(2) *Schedule these items.* If these items on your list are important, they should be given a place on your schedule on a regular basis, at least weekly.

(3) *Put the items in the time slots in which they fit best.* At work you may have to spend most of your time taking care of boss-imposed and system-imposed matters. But schedule time for self-imposed items that enable you to work ahead on projects that are important but not urgent. Away from work, apply the same principle. Take care of immediate needs as required, but schedule time to work ahead on items that are important but not immediately urgent.[21]

The Sabbath, the various seasonal festivals in ancient Israel, and the year of Jubilee were all ways of putting on the Israelites' schedules activities for focusing again on what was important in life. Israel was not to live by routine nor let things follow their natural course. Rather, Israel was to live by and for a purpose. We would do well to learn from their experience. Without a conscious effort to identify and schedule priorities, we find ourselves going through the motions of life ever more quickly but without moving toward a destination.

Evaluate regularly the way you manage your time.

Use the beginning of each week, perhaps Sunday afternoon or evening, to review the roles in your life that you believe are important and to consider what you are going to do about each of those roles in the coming week. Does a spouse, a child, or an aging parent need attention? What do you need to do to be of service as a person of faith? What growth or recreation activities do you need to plan for yourself? You might already have used the last block of time you had the previous Friday afternoon to plan for the coming week at work, reviewing appointments you have scheduled and items you intend to get done.

In the case of both work time and away-from-work time, your goal should be to identify and work on the important items, the items that get results toward achieving your purpose in life. Important items come in two packages. One package is marked "urgent"; we have no choice other than to work on these items. The other package of important items is marked "not yet urgent." Stephen Covey is right on target in suggesting that the best time management calls for working more and more on the important items that are not yet urgent.[22] Being able to work on such items enables us to be more and more in control of our time and thus have our lives in balance. We get out of the "react to crisis" mode; we get into the mode of planning ahead to prevent crises, identify new opportunities, and expand our horizons.

Each day, perhaps at the end of the day, perhaps at the beginning of the day, reserve some time for reviewing what you've accomplished, planning for the coming day, and making whatever adjustments are needed from the week's plan you developed at the beginning of the week. One crucially important way of connecting your work with your faith is to include this development and review of your schedule and to-do list in your daily time of devotion and prayer. This includes reviewing your work calendar as well as your away-from-work calendar.

In addition to these daily and weekly planning times, at least one other technique is helpful. Use the beginning of the year or some other significant time to take a broad look at how you're doing in achieving your life purposes. Identify what you'd like to accomplish in the coming year or other period of time. Make some specific plans for accomplishing these goals, and include them as a part of your weekly planning.

So When Are You Going to Get Serious about Balancing Your Life?

Want a balanced life, a life without rushing, a life where you are able to spend the time necessary to take care of all the important things, a life where you feel in control?

It's hard to feel that we're living the abundant life faith provides when incessant demands on our time are draining away our energy and we feel out of control. Why don't you put these ideas into practice, then? They're an avenue toward living your faith, including in the world of work.

Notes

[1]Geoffrey Godbey and Alan Graefe, "Rapid Growth in Rushin' Americans," *American Demographics* (April 1993): 26, 28, citing studies by the National Recreation and Park Association and the Americans' Use of Time Project.

[2]Juliet B. Schor, *The Overworked American: The Unexpected Decline of Leisure* (New York: Basic Books, 1991) 2.

[3]Ibid.

[4]Ibid., 29.

[5]Ibid., 31.

[6]Ibid.

[7]Ibid., 86-88.

[8]Harriet B. Braiker, *The Type E* Woman: How to Overcome the Stress of Being *Everything to Everybody* (New York: Dodd, Mead & Co., 1986) 7.

[9]Charlie Hochschild, with Anne Machung, *The Second Shift: Working Parents and the Revolution at Home* (New York: Viking Press, 1989) 6.

[10]William Oncken, Jr., *Managing Management Time* (Englewood Cliffs NJ: Prentice-Hall, 1984) 76-87.

[11]For additional suggestions about using time at work most effectively, see my previous book, *How to Be Happier in the Job You Sometimes Can't Stand* (Nashville TN: Broadman Press, 1990) chapter 7, "Get Organized." For additional suggestions about balancing life, see chapter 9, "Live with Balance."

[12]Karl Albrecht, *Brain Power: Learn to Improve Your Thinking Skills* (Englewood Cliffs NJ: Prentice-Hall, 1980) 5. Albrecht's image comes to mind each time I see him on television now, unfortunately!

[13]R. David Thomas, "How to Add by Subtracting," *Higher Than the Top* (Nashville TN: Dimensions for Living, 1993) 86-87.

[14]John Cowan, *Small Decencies: Reflections and Mediations on Being Human at Work* (New York: HarperBusiness, 1992) 55.

[15]Merrill E. Douglass and Donna N. Douglass, *Manage Your Time, Your Work, Yourself,* updated edition (New York: AMACOM, 1993) 152.

[16]Marian Wright Edelman, *The Measure of Our Success: A Letter to My Children and Yours* (New York: HarperPerennial, 1992) 70.

[17]Douglass and Douglass, 157.

[18]Oncken, 2-4.

[19]An obvious exception would be a Maytag® repair technician.

[20]Joseph Juran, quoted in Barbara Ettore, "Juran on Quality," *Management Review* (January 1994):11.

[21]For excellent assistance in this area, see Stephen R. Covey, *The Seven Habits of Highly Effective People: Restoring the Character Ethic* (New York: Simon & Schuster, 1989) 144-82.

[22]Ibid., 151.

Chapter 9
Lighten Up

"COONHUNTERS FOR CHRIST." Believe it or not, that's the bumper sticker I saw on a pickup truck when I exited from a restaurant that featured down-home cooking. I suppose the person who put the bumper sticker on the truck might not see the humor in it, and perhaps avowed coonhunters might not see the humor in it, but I did. Really, wouldn't you agree that "Coonhunters for Christ" is a tad more droll than, say, "Accountants for Christ" or "Engineers for Christ"?

Let me say that I do not mean with these remarks to offend accountants, engineers, professional or amateur coonhunters, hunters of anything legal, or drivers of pickup trucks. Some of my best friends are accountants and engineers. Some more of my friends are coonhunters, or at least used to be. I've been known to hunt on occasion myself. Definitely, many of my best friends and many of my family members drive pickup trucks. I actually do not know whether my remarks fit in or out of the "politically correct" category I keep hearing about.

The point is—well—could we all just lighten up a little? What would be so wrong with that? Christians of all people, unfortunately, need to lighten up. Too many Christians are entirely too serious—everywhere, but especially out in public on their jobs. Many coworkers of such people consider them to be too judgmental, too critical, too, too serious, and not the least bit interested in anything resembling fun. They feel we're just too good, so good that we're "goody-two-shoes" folks who stand in judgment on people who don't measure up to our standard of righteousness. They think we're like how we think the Pharisees were. In many cases, that evaluation is dead-on right.

People of faith need to lighten up a bit, and it's entirely possible to do so while still being serious about living faith in the world of work. Here are some ways it can be done.

Remember the Inadequacies of Puritanism as *the* Definition of Faith

The Puritans—God rest their souls—were serious people of faith. Seriousness, though, was more of a vice than a virtue for them. The Puritans seem to have defined seriousness a bit too broadly. As a former church history professor of mine suggested, they gave the distinct impression that God would be unhappy—and certainly they would be sad—if anybody ever had any fun. That sort of impression has been passed down rather handily in American Christianity. Many people of faith have had that impression impressed upon them a little too deeply.

Management consultant John Cowan tells of being in a small airport where the pilot of a single-engine airplane was practicing touch-and-go landings and takeoffs. Cowan sat where he could see the runway and observe the plane's maneuvers. A mother with a young girl about seven years old and a little boy about five were also in the room. The children, though, had their backs to the runway. Lured by the excitement outside, however, the children gradually turned around to watch the airplane. The mother became aware of what the children were doing. Though the children were not harming or bothering anyone, she said to them, "Turn around and sit up straight." Cowan comments, "I hate that woman to this day. I still grieve for her children."[1]

Being ordered to turn around and sit up straight when there's no reason to do so and when we in so doing miss the fun of life illustrates the inadequacy of Puritanism as an approach to faith. We would be wise never to forget the wonders of childhood. And if we've forgotten that, I crave for all forgetful people to know the wonders of grandparenthood. There's no substitute for hearing a little voice saying, "Granddad, Granddad, come play with me." (Did I tell you about my wonderful grandchildren yet?)

We would also be wise never to forget that we are all still children. A little child lives in each of us; that little child doesn't go away when we become people of faith, though we may stifle the little voice. I advise you never to tell that child, "Turn around and sit up straight," when to keep looking at the airplane would bring joy and hurt no one. There are appropriate times and places even at work to remember and acknowledge that perception.

The Hebrews knew the value of a life of joy. People unfamiliar with the Bible tend to assume that in those days people of faith spent their days in sackcloth and ashes, confessing their sins, and that their religion was drab drudgery. (Believe me, drab drudgery would be close to the ultimate in drudgery. I know; I've been there, done that.)

Actually, a great amount of Hebrew religion was celebration. Some of the feasts, in fact, were rather rip-roaring celebrations. Everybody came, made sacrifices of animals by cooking them medium-well to well-done, shared some of the food with the religious leaders, and ate most of the rest themselves. It was a family reunion, a Saturday barbecue, and what folks where I grew up called "all-day dinner and singing on the grounds." Those Hebrews surely knew how to have fun *and* worship God at the same time.

So did Jesus. One of the judgments the religious leaders of Jesus' day made against him was that he seemed to party an awful lot. Worse, he partied with the wrong people, people who weren't nearly as strait-laced as the religious leaders felt everybody ought to be.

Too-serious people of faith would be wise to evaluate whether they're more like the Puritans than they need to be. Me, I'll take Jesus as the model.

Learn to Laugh, Though Not at Others' Expense

"A thing of beauty," the poet said, "is a joy forever." So is hearty laughter when it is not at someone else's expense. Laughter may be the next best thing to prayer, for laughter gets people in touch with things other than the cares of time.

Laughter comes from our brain's surprised and delighted recognition that we, smart as we are, are limited. Laughter acknowledges our humanity and recognizes that we have been fooled. Logic suggested that the next word or the next event would be one thing, but something else, something unexpected and out of the ordinary, occurred. If the Puritans had known that laughter was such serious business, maybe they would have laughed more.

Business executive Max DePree states an important truth for people of faith in the world of work, or anywhere else for that matter: "You'll find a sense of humor essential to living with ambiguity."[2] And that's what we have to do in life—live with ambiguity, with things that aren't all figured out or logical.

Humor is one of the attributes that Robert Greenleaf included as an essential for the optimum lifestyle.[3] Why? Because recognizing and dealing appropriately with ambiguity and even absurdity is a part of life, including life at work, perhaps especially life at work.

Who has not marveled at the seeming stupidity of certain actions taken at work, perhaps ordered by management. What is euphemistically and mistakenly called "communication" through line management in a good-sized corporation is an example. A simple request by the CEO becomes a massive, time-consuming crash program for dozens if not hundreds of employees, for example. On many occasions, communication through line management resembles the parlor game of "gossip" more than anything else. Many CEOs would be amazed if they ever found out how little the message the employee on the shop floor received resembles the message the CEO intended to send. I predict that if you work for a large corporation or for the government, you've experienced such a joyful time yourself.

In a place at which I formerly worked, there lived the legend of "Management Man," which probably should have been "Management Person," except that no woman likely would mind not being included in Management Man's work. What did Management Man do? The story goes that Management Man would spend his days moving through the corporation. When Management Man found things going well, with happy employees operating at a high level of productivity for the benefit of satisfied customers, Management Man would take the following actions immediately: say, "I'll fix that"; slip into a closet; rip off his coat, tie, and shirt, thus revealing a red, yellow, and blue "Management Man" T-shirt (like you-know-who's); emerge from the closet; and then proceed to foul up the situation.

I never saw Management Man personally, but I've seen his handi-work many times. I know that Management Man must be real because the people who reported to me when I was in management gave me a Management Man T-shirt. I tried always to keep it handy during my management career.

Retired publishing executive James Autry tells of the humorous events he participated in and sometimes instigated that brought levity to the workplace. Such events went a long way toward making it more human and humane. For example, one of the sources of unhappiness among workers in the building was the lack of air conditioning. Autry tells of singing a carol to the tune of "The Twelve Days of Christmas." This new edition of the carol closed with the line, "Give us fewer vice presidents and more air conditioning."[4] Who in the lower rungs of the workplace has not wanted to sing a song like that, and how many company presidents have wanted to sing it, too?

I myself have been known to use humor at times, though not in this book, in case you are about to search the pages for it. Unbeliev-ably to many who know me, I've been known by some others as a halfway witty person. In fact, when I was demonstrating this ability in an official meeting with people outside my company, one person laughed and asked me what the management of my company thought about it. I said, well, I still work there. I should say now that I no longer work there.

Of course, many things happen at work at which if we did not laugh, we would cry. Laughter seems to be more socially acceptable than tears in most work settings. However, I confess that I once tried humor to lighten up a situation when my boss was engaging me in a conversation that turned out to be more serious than I thought—a *lot* more serious. I do not recommend lightening up in such a situation, especially if your boss's first name is composed of only three letters. (I'd just like to say that if my former boss is reading this and thinks it's him, let me assure him that it may be the other boss whose name also was composed of only three letters. Anyway, I no longer work at either place, and so what does it matter which one I'm talking about? So just lighten up, okay?

People of faith are people who are in touch with eternity and not merely with the demands of the moment. They also recognize their own limitations. So they have more reason to laugh than anyone else. Laughter is an important part of faith.

Recognize Your Imperfections/ Allow Other People Their Differences

Jesus spoke rather plainly about the order in which people ought to recognize and deal with imperfections. The order for judging and criticizing people is ourselves first, and then others only after we've finished improving ourselves. Jesus put it this way (Matt 7:3): "Why do you see the speck in your neighbor's eye, but do not notice the log in your own eye?" Christians could correct their image of being judgmental and critical by putting this teaching into practice.

Recognizing our imperfections also provides a basis for listening to others and giving fair consideration to their ideas rather than assuming that as people of faith our ideas are universally superior and provide the quintessential model for successful living. Humility is a Christian virtue, remember?

Diversity training is important in the business world today. Diversity training, in addition to avoiding lawsuits, aims at helping all the employees of a company to accept and work with each other for the total good of the company, even though they may differ in gender, race, and other qualities.

People of genuine faith ought to be ahead of the game in treating fairly, kindly, even lovingly, people in the world of work who are different from them. People of faith ought to be the company specialists in doing the right things in relationships with people—all people—at work. It's the law, of course, but it's also the right thing to do. Lightening up means growing to be as accepting of people in all their diversity as a loving God is.

The Results of Lightening Up

Here are some results of lightening up as a way of living faith in the world of work:

• You'll be a better advertisement for faith and help to overcome some of the negative public relations that people of faith have, largely through their own fault.
• You will be better able to deal with stress.
• You'll probably live longer, if you don't get run over by a car with an "I ❤ Jesus" bumper sticker on its bumper and a radar detector on the dash.

Notes

[1]John Cowan, *Small Decencies: Reflections and Meditations on Being Human at Work* (New York: HarperBusiness, 1992) 56.

[2]Max DePree, *Leadership Jazz* (New York: Dell Publishing, 1992) 222.

[3]Robert K. Greenleaf, *Servant Leadership: A Journey into the Nature of Legitimate Power and Greatness* (New York: Paulist Press, 1977) 298.

[4]James A. Autry, *Life and Work: A Manager's Search for Meaning* (New York: William Morrow & Co., 1994) 27.

Chapter 10
Practice Personal Disciplines for Integrating Work with Faith

What personal actions and qualities are needed within for living faith in the world of work? The tendency of current American religion is to respond to such a question by listing three, ten, or a dozen easy steps to success.[1] On the positive side, the call to come up with such a list represents a legitimate desire to figure out what we need to do to get to the goal we seek. There's a lot to be said for that. The negative side comes into play when we take the list as a set of rules, do the tasks suggested, and yet fail to care about getting the meaning behind them into our lives.

It is possible to take the disciplines suggested in this chapter merely as some tasks to be done, some rules to be kept. There is probably some value in doing that, for these disciplines can be powerful in their effects, especially over time. Doing these disciplines employs the valid psychological principle of changing behavior first so feelings and attitudes will change as a result of the change in behavior. Still, you likely will get even more value from the disciplines described in this chapter if you recognize the purpose behind them and cooperate consciously with that purpose.

So what is the purpose behind practicing these personal disciplines? These disciplines are meant to lead to a clear-eyed self-awareness of who you are and how you're operating at work and elsewhere. They're meant to get you in touch on a regular, ongoing basis with your soul and with the God of your soul. If you do that, you will live with an awareness of who you are and what you're doing at each moment in time, including your time at work, rather than simply playing an expected role and going through the motions—like painting by the numbers. You will respond and live in an honest relationship with yourself, your fellow human beings, and God.

Such self-awareness comes from only one source: the development of the inner life. While there are some steps to be taken in this direction, they're not easy. Too, even when you take these steps consistently, you will never really be able to check them off your list and say, "There; that's done." So here are a few powerful but not-so-easy personal disciplines to practice if you're serious about wanting to live your faith in the world of work.

Spend Time Each Day in Prayer and Meditation

On one of my early trips to New York City, I persuaded a friend to be adventurous and take the subway with me from our hotel near Times Square down to the World Trade Center. We did just that. After all, why waste a perfectly good Sunday afternoon in the Big Apple just because we had little money, didn't know our way around, and had heard all sorts of stories about the dangers of New York City, especially the subway? I couldn't think of a good reason either. So we went.

Our trip to the World Trade Center and to the top went without a hitch. We enjoyed the spectacular view and then began the journey back to our hotel. As we were preparing to get on the subway for the return trip, however, some sixth sense told me that if we boarded the subway from that platform we would be going the wrong direction, toward Battery Park rather than back toward Times Square. I motioned to my friend to come with me, and we crossed over to the other side. Soon a train came, we boarded it, and we were back on our way to our hotel.

My friend marveled at how I was able to perform this delicate operation so well (almost get us lost and then recover?). I'm not sure how myself, but all my life I have trained myself to be aware of where I am geographically and which direction I am heading. I'm sure it goes back to my boyhood days playing in the pine woods of my home area in very rural Louisiana. Some sort of learning must have transferred all the way from the logging roads in the woods to the subway, I suppose. Although I have on relatively rare occasions become disoriented—okay, lost—my sense of direction has served me quite well through the years.

How about a sense of direction in life, including life at work? Where do you get that? I don't know of a better way to maintain your sense of direction in life, including life at work, than through regular meditation and prayer. Your faith then becomes your North Star, capable of providing guidance through any day and any circumstance.

In a previous chapter, I suggested a pattern for beginning or ending the day that called for a combination of prayer, Bible study, and planning time for one's life at work and away from work. Such a pattern provides a way of staying in touch, we might say, with both heaven and earth, especially of bringing heaven's resources together with earth's demands.

I encourage you to try doing this yourself. Find a devotional resource that offers guidance in study and devotion, preferably based on the Scriptures. Let that activity serve as a springboard to your daily calendar. In the intersection between the message of the Scriptures and the obligations and opportunities of your daily calendar, listen for God's guidance and encouragement for the day. Use that time, too, to pray for your coworkers and the events at work in which you will be involved. Perhaps, too, as you move through the day, as opportunities permit and obligations demand, ask yourself what you're doing in that very moment and how what you find yourself doing is in line with God's message of guidance, encouragement, and, perhaps, reprimand, to you.

Jesus' model applies to us in our life at work as in other times and places. Helmut Thielicke, in his classic book on Jesus' parables, wrote eloquently about Jesus:

> Why was it that he spoke with authority, as the scribes and Pharisees did not? Because he was rhetorically gifted, because he was dynamic? No; he spoke with such power because he had first spoken with the Father, because always he came out of silence. He rested in eternity and therefore broke into time with such power. That's why he is so disturbing to time. He lived in communion with God.[2]

Our own coming "out of silence" into the rush-rush, high-pressure world of work will give us the power needed within for both doing our jobs in the world of work and living our faith while we do them. Elton Trueblood put the need for spiritual communication with the God of our souls in proper perspective when he wrote: "Much as we may need to pray when we are in church, we often need to pray far more when we are engaged in difficult mental or manual tasks" at our jobs.[3]

Philip Crosby, the total quality management leader, recommends that people whose business is having difficulty take a number of specific business actions to solve the problem. One word of advice seems particularly unbusinesslike, but Crosby expresses it adamantly and forthrightly:

> Pray. The Lord takes a hand in the affairs of business when asked. Start each meeting with a word of thanks for taking the specific action that has been requested. Make Him a full partner and don't apologize for it to anyone.[4]

You may or may not find doing this appropriate in public in your own business setting, but the point is clear. Our work, our jobs, deserve our prayers just as much as any other aspect of our lives.

While in Washington, D.C., on business, I was on my way to my morning appointment at the National Geographic Society a couple of blocks away from my hotel. It was winter, and ice and snow covered the streets and sidewalks. Then I saw something so representative of the problem of spiritual communication of so many people today.

Walking along, I saw something unusual embedded in the ice at the curb. My thoughts went from "What could it be?" to "Could it be?" to "Yes, it is" to "That's unbelievable." What was it? It was a beeper, that ubiquitous modern symbol of our desire and our need to stay in touch with others, for business reasons.

I wonder how the person who lost his beeper to the ice fared that day. Perhaps better than do many people who have lost or misplaced their spiritual beepers. The person who lost his beeper in the ice probably lost only a day of contact with people who needed to get in touch with him, some urgently perhaps. People who lose or misplace their spiritual beepers, their spiritual contact with God, lose the opportunity to be in touch with the God of their souls and to receive God's message of encouragement, hope, and challenge. . . . What's that I hear from that snowdrift? Could it be for you? Better check in.

Take Good Care of Yourself Physically

A number of years ago I heard an outstanding preacher named Howard Thurman preach. It's hard for me to remember most of my own sermons, and so the fact that I've remembered for years something Dr. Thurman said means there was something significant about him and his message. At the time I heard him, he had already served as Dean of the Chapel at Boston University and Howard University. He also ministered in other significant places of service, including founding and serving as pastor of the Church for the Fellowship of All Peoples in San Francisco. *Life* magazine named him one of the twentieth century's greatest preachers.

Dr. Thurman told of going to his physician for his regular checkup. After the checkup, the physician informed Dr. Thurman that everything was fine, but he needed to lose about ten pounds. The preacher told how he reacted. He knew the physician was right and that he did indeed need to lose the ten pounds.

Dr. Thurman said he couldn't help noticing, however, that his physician was at least fifty pounds overweight himself. Thurman pondered how his physician could advise him to lose ten pounds when obviously the physician himself needed to lose fifty. How could the physician not know that he himself needed to lose the excessive weight?

Without asking the physician, Dr. Thurman then came to this conclusion. The physician evidently thought his body knew he was a physician and that knowledge somehow exempted him from following the rules of health. Thurman commented: "But my doctor's body did not know he was a doctor. And your body doesn't know you're an important person either."

Whoever you yourself are, however important your position at work is, however good a person you are, however many people you help, however many degrees you have, however strongly you believe in God, and however much you know and practice your faith, your body doesn't know any of that about you. Your body knows only the importance of proper nutrition, exercise, and rest to keep this body that is so "fearfully and wonderfully made" working properly (Ps 139:14). The body is not able to make an exception for you when you refuse to live in accord with good nutrition, exercise, and rest. That's not the way bodily functions are set up to operate.

In the life of the body as in the life of farming, we do reap what we sow. If we insist on refusing to follow the guidelines of good health, we may well have to pay a price. Of course, a part of the problem is that refusing to follow these guidelines doesn't result in immediate, recognizable consequences we can connect with whatever we did or didn't do. It would be easier always to eat the right food, for example, if the consequences of not doing so were immediate and visible. If when we ate a high-cholesterol food such as fettucine alfredo (referred to as "heart attack on a plate") for example, six-inch high bumps arose on our foreheads, we probably would avoid that food next time. I would. Fortunately or unfortunately, we've been entrusted with greater discretionary powers, even if we don't use them.

Many companies have long recognized the importance of encouraging physical health among employees. For one thing, employees who maintain good health tend to be able to produce more for the company. In addition, of course, maintaining good health minimizes health care costs.

The motivation for people of faith to take good care of themselves physically goes even beyond the physical and the vocational, of course. Refusing to follow good health habits costs spiritually as well as physically. How we feel we're doing spiritually often connects closely with how we're actually doing physically. When the prophet Elijah was so depressed about his seeming ineffectiveness, a good sleep and something good to eat—not too much, and it wasn't fettucine alfredo! —were steps toward his recovery, aided by an angel (1 Kgs 19:4-8).

Keep Growing Mentally

Studies of how we think and don't think have revealed a disturbing truth. This information explains a lot of things about the kind of thinking we and others sometimes do. Here's the disturbing truth: The more times we think a certain thought or think in a certain way, the more likely it is we will do that again. Why? What difference does it make?

Take the "why" question first. Electrical pathways are worn in our brains when we think in a certain way. When we repeat that sort of thinking, the pathway deepens, so to speak, and the electrical connections increase in strength. Each time we think in that manner, in fact, the pathway becomes more clearly defined. As a result, it becomes much easier for the next thought to follow the same path and much harder for a new thought or a new kind of thinking to occur. Thus, like water following the path of least resistance, thoughts also follow the path of least resistance as they are being formed.[5]

What difference does that make? It's an uphill battle for most of us to continue to grow mentally. We get into habits in our thinking. We prefer to think the old thoughts or to think in the old ways, which is so comfortable we may miss new possibilities that would provide new and better results. We become the people who say, "I've seen lots of changes in my time here, and I've been against them all." Both reputed liberals and reputed conservatives can trap themselves into such thinking.

Frightening as it is to think new thoughts or to think thoughts in new ways, the combination of closed-mindedness and a reputation as a person of faith is deadening. Accurately or inaccurately, this is the impression many people have of people of faith, in fact. Having faith in God means having convictions, of course, but it doesn't mean that we stop thinking, stop learning, or changing in response to new circumstances and new information.

The person—person of faith or not—who refuses to think a new way has one of two problems and perhaps both simultaneously. He is either so unsure of his current ideas that he's afraid to have them challenged or so egotistical he believes he already knows everything there is to know, thank you. Besides, it's so simple, anyone who thinks otherwise must be really stupid.

So how do we keep from getting into ruts in our thinking? (I'm assuming, of course, that the ruts are not so deep in our minds already that we're unable to consider this thought.) Here are some things you can do:

(1) *Keep learning, both formally and informally.* Take classes, read, listen to other people—yes, listen to other people.

(2) *Force yourself to use this new learning to expand your perspective, not merely to confirm your current ideas.* Someone suggested that most people use facts only to confirm and support their prejudices. That kind of thinking is not good enough for people of faith.

(3) *Do this learning in settings beyond your own culture or comfortable set of ideas.* The world is a whole lot bigger than our small valley. Read things you don't ordinarily read. Talk to people whose perspective is different from yours, and try to understand their position (the Golden Rule).

(4) *Go behind the labels to the reality.* "Labelitis" is an unfortunate, often undiagnosed disease that affects many people's minds. Labelitis is a thinking shortcut that looks like thinking but is not thinking. Labelitis kills thinking.

The person afflicted with labelitis quickly attaches a label to an idea and either buys or rejects it solely on the basis of the label, without thinking. What do labels such as religious, secular, liberal, conservative, traditional, or New Age really tell about the idea or action itself? The label serves merely as a shorthand way of categorizing the idea without taking the time or making the effort to consider it. Labelitis is bumper-sticker thinking.

Labels don't tell the whole truth. Far from it. Just because some idea is labeled "religious" doesn't mean it is. Just because an idea is described as "liberal" or "conservative" doesn't mean there's no truth in it. Just because some process at work is "the way we've always done it" does not mean it's the best way now, given new technology and new competitive realities.

(5) *Recognize the place that paradigms play in our thinking.* The word "paradigm" has come into rather wide use in business to describe a way of looking at various aspects of the business world.

What is a paradigm? A paradigm basically is a viewpoint on a certain set of circumstances. It's meant to explain these circumstances so actions can be taken based on that explanation. It's a viewpoint on reality. Often, however, a paradigm is not recognized for what it is— a way of looking at reality rather than reality itself. Furthermore, paradigms are inadequate. They do not take account of all the facts. Paradigms are simply the best we can do in our thinking at the time.[6]

For example, once the world operated by the paradigm that the earth was flat. The discovery by the European world that continents existed that were unknown to them forced development of a new paradigm. Progress is made only when people recognize the shortcomings of particular paradigms and dare to suggest that a new way of viewing —thinking about—the situation may be in order.

Both the world of faith and the world of business get caught in inadequate paradigms and often fail to recognize the inadequacies of these paradigms. A principle that has been used forever—meaning for the past few years—is assumed to be perfect and unquestionable. Such as? "A woman can't do this job—or shouldn't be doing this job." A process that has been in place for several years may be defended as being incapable of improvement. "That's the way we've always done it, and it's worked just fine." But that process may be technologically out-of-date, or the business's competitors may have moved far beyond it. People of faith ought to lead the way in thinking in all aspects of their lives, not be viewed as people who refuse to think fresh thoughts, either in their faith or in their business.

(6) *Focus on facts and reasons, not just impressions about "the way we've done it in the past."* An important method used in implementing total quality management in business is actually to find out what customers want. What a radical thought! What happens next? The company can then gear its actions to provide customers what they want or else explain why the company is unable to do it and suggest alternatives that will still meet the customers' needs.

Total quality management also is about actually finding out how a process needs to be improved or what new processes need to be created. The goal is improving rather than continuing to operate in the most familiar and comfortable manner, certain that we know the answers. The same kind of rigorous attention to facts provides the foundation for improvement in all areas of life.

A word of caution: Most of us can be rather selective about facts, choosing to give credence only to those that justify our position. Watch it. Another word of caution: We never have all the facts. In addition to the suggestions in this section, use the pointers in chapter 5 to check out decisions, especially those that involve ethical matters.

*****

Keep growing mentally. People of faith need to emphasize this personal discipline. We'll make a greater contribution to both the world of faith and the world of business, as well as the world of family and all our other worlds, if we will. In addition, we'll overcome the bad reputation that people of faith have, and all too often deserve—that they don't think. Before all else fails, think.

Avoid Letting Money Dominate Your Life

When Malcolm Forbes, one of the world's richest people, died, his friends said he was a wonderful man who had meant much to Wall Street and who had lived life to the hilt. For his seventieth birthday a few months before his death, Forbes had flown a thousand guests to Morocco for his birthday party. It's said that he spent a couple of million dollars on the occasion. He was a very wealthy man, and he enjoyed spending the money he had earned and accumulated.

Today, however, although I do not know your financial circumstances, I can guarantee that you are richer in material things than Malcolm Forbes. You may have borrowed this book instead of purchased it, but I can still guarantee that you have more material things than Malcolm Forbes.

Stocks, bonds, real estate, bank accounts, and dollars don't matter to Mr. Forbes today. You can't take it with you, and neither could Mr. Forbes, rich as he was. Nobody can. How much did Mr. Forbes leave? We didn't have to wait until the attorneys and the accountants figured it up and the relatives transferred it to their accounts to learn how much he left. He left it all. Every bit of it. All.

I know little of the character of Malcolm Forbes, the kind of person he was. I'll leave that judgment to Mr. Forbes' family and friends and to God. For all I know, Malcolm Forbes was truly a wonderful and good man, just as many people said he was. I have no reason to think otherwise.

But today I'm more impressed with someone else. They, too, are richer than Mr. Forbes today. They, however, were richer than he was any day he was alive as well. I'm sure of this evaluation, even though Ruth once pointed to thirteen trunks that had just been shipped from Africa and said, "Those are all our worldly possessions." She and her husband Bert spent their adult lives working with the people of two African nations, Nigeria and Sierra Leone. Bert and Ruth are gifted, educated, caring, generous, competent, *good* people. My hunch is they would be successful, perhaps even monetarily, wherever and however they chose to spend their lives.

If worldly possessions were the real measure of quality in people, Bert and Ruth deserve all that Malcolm Forbes had and more. Instead, they came to retirement—early, for health reasons—and all their worldly possessions were in thirteen trunks. No house, no land, probably little money. They depended on their pensions for their livelihood. But they were wealthy. As missionaries, Bert and Ruth invested their lives in people, giving of themselves without reserve.

Friends of mine who visited the couple both in Nigeria and in Sierra Leone, agree unanimously:

> You cannot imagine how revered Bert and Ruth are among the people where they lived and worked. Everywhere we went the people spoke in tones of reverence, respect, and gratitude for them. You cannot imagine the impact of their lives on those people.

Another friend who had visited them in Nigeria reported that the people referred to Bert as the "big man" because of the greatness of his contributions. Quite a legacy.

Malcolm Forbes and Bert and Ruth. With no disrespect intended toward Mr. Forbes, there's no comparison in my mind about the best way to spend a life. Had you rather your life be represented by those thirteen trunks or by a billion dollars? Don't be foolish. Ask Malcolm Forbes if you ever get a chance. He'll tell you the wisest course. Take the trunks.

People who let money dominate their lives sometimes decide to do things for money that in their heart of hearts they know is not best. They may bend their integrity to keep their job. After all, they have a mortgage payment to meet. They may go so far as to engage in shady business practices in order to make a little or a lot of money. It's not exactly like robbing a bank, but the "principle" is the same, isn't it?

In a previous chapter, we looked at how we could work half the hours we work today if we were willing to live with the same material standard of living the nation had in 1948.[7] We pay the price for material things not just in dollars but in time and stress. Perhaps we should pay more attention to this proverb from the Bible: "Do not wear yourself out to get rich; be wise enough to desist" (Prov 23:4).

Regular surveys since the 1950s indicate that the portion of the United States population who describe themselves as "very happy" has hovered at about the same level all through the years—one-third. This consistent pattern has occurred at the same time that the material standard of living has been rising quite dramatically.[8] Evidently money really doesn't buy happiness.

Plenty of references in the Bible indicate the importance of refusing to let money dominate our lives. The book of Ecclesiastes, for example, warns of the emptiness of money as the ultimate goal of life. Ecclesiastes 5:10 states that money will not satisfy. Indeed, as material goods increase, desire for material goods also increases, leaving a person endlessly unsatisfied and still questing for more (5:11).

Proverbs 28:6 calls people to set their priorities on the right things, stating that it is, "better to be poor and walk in integrity than to be crooked in one's ways even though rich." Another passage in Proverbs acknowledges in a prayer the captivating power of material things, asking,

> Remove far from me falsehood and lying, give me neither poverty nor riches; feed me with the food that I need, or I shall be full, and deny you, and say, "Who is the Lord?" or I shall be poor, and steal, and profane the name of my God. (30:8-9)

Jesus also called for refusing to allow money to dominate one's life. In the Sermon on the Mount, he commanded that his followers stop trying to accumulate "treasures on earth" and taught about the perishable nature of material things (Matt 6:19-21). He also pointed out the impossibility of attempting to serve two masters—God and mammon, God and material things (v. 24). Not only should people of faith not try to serve both God and material wealth, but doing so is simply impossible, in fact.

In an unforgettable parable, Jesus taught the foolishness of thinking that our lives "consist in the abundance of possessions" (Luke 12:15). The parable is the story of a man who miscalculated seriously the answers to these questions (see Luke 12:13-21):

• Who owns material things?
• Do I use material things for higher purposes, or do material things own me?
• How long do I have to live?
• How much is enough?

These questions continue to give us difficulty, too. The final one is especially hard. When most people, including people of faith, are asked, "How much is enough?" they respond, "Only a little more."

What we have is too much and too expensive if we have to sacrifice values and relationships to reach such a standard of living. A professor and his family moved from a smaller house with one bath to a larger house with two baths. The professor's eleven-year-old son made a telling remark that revealed much about priorities. Missing his friends, the boy informed his parents that he had rather have two friends than two baths! Allowing for the aversion of some boys to baths, I'd still say he had his priorities in order. He knew the answer to the question, "How much is enough?" Having enough is having needs and wants met while preserving values more important than money.

The Scriptures recognize that some people will be so blessed materially that they can have more than enough without sacrificing important values. In 1 Timothy 6:17-19, Paul provides instructions to such people, commanding them

> not to be haughty, or to set their hopes on the uncertainty of riches, but rather on God who richly provides us with everything for our enjoyment. They are to do good, to be rich in good works, generous, and ready to share, thus storing up for themselves the treasure of a good foundation for the future, so that they may take hold of the life that really is life.

This advice applies to many people of faith in America, who are rich by the standards of the rest of the world.

The theologian Dietrich Bonhoeffer reminded us, "Earthly goods are given to be used, not to be collected."[9] So, rather than allowing the money we have to dominate our lives, we are to earn it in accord with our highest values and use it for the greatest purposes.

What are the greatest purposes for which money can be used? Theologian Richard Foster suggests that Jesus' command to lay up treasure in heaven instead of on earth can be understood by considering what will be in heaven. The answer is people. So, he suggests,

> The proper use of money is not for living high down here; that would be a very poor investment indeed. No, the proper use of money is for investing as much of it as possible in the lives of people, so that we will have treasure in heaven.[10]

Paul may have summed up most of the advice people need about money in his message to the church at Ephesus on his last visit there. He said,

> You know for yourselves that I worked with my own hands to support myself and my companions. In all this I have given you an example that by such work we must support the weak, remembering the words of the Lord Jesus, for he himself said, "It is more blessed to give than to receive." (Acts 20:34-35)

Such behavior provides a strong positive example about how to stop letting money dominate our lives.

To avoid letting money dominate your life, evaluate how you are getting it and how you are using it by these questions:

• To what extent am I able to maintain my highest values in my work, the way in which I earn my livelihood?
• To what extent do I use my money to help others?

Work to the Best of Your Ability

This is the homespun description of a certain person in the community in which I grew up: "He was never much to work." He was quite active in church. Still, the perception that he did not work, much less to the best of his ability, lessened the positive influence he could have had in that hard-working community.

People who are serious about living their faith in the world of work will be known as workers as well as believers. A biblical proverb advises of the serious consequences of failing to work to the best of one's ability: "One who is slack in work is close kin to a vandal" (Prov 18:9).

In the New Testament, Paul also called for diligence in work. He wrote these words:

Whatever your task, put yourselves into it, as done for the Lord and not for your masters, since you know that from the Lord you will receive the inheritance as your reward; you serve the Lord Christ. (Col 3:23-24)

Moreover, Paul instructed slaves to obey their masters "not only while being watched, and in order to please them, but as slaves of Christ, doing the will of God from the heart" (Eph 6:6). Although the social circumstances are different today, this teaching still translates powerfully into the present world of work. Genuine faith demands diligence in work even when one's supervisor is not looking.

So, what is the first responsibility of the person of faith in the world of work? Simply, to work diligently at one's job. In fact, attention to the work provides a positive witness in itself of one's seriousness in living faith in the workplace. The work contains value in itself. The job is not merely what one does to be able to do something else after work.

A central teaching of the Shaker sect may have captured the ideal connection of faith and work. The Shakers summarized that connection in a sort of motto, "Hands to work, hearts to God." This thought recognized that the life of faith included both work and worship. Diligent work at one's job is as much a part of the life of faith as fervent worship, even when one fails to see much eternal significance in the results of the work.

So, the cobbler who said that his business was saving souls but that he repaired shoes to pay expenses may not have had the best evaluation of his work, no matter how noble his sentiments were. His first responsibility—to God as well as to the people who brought shoes to him—was to repair his customers' shoes and to do it well.

Furthermore, people of faith must not only work diligently, but they also must continue to grow in their ability to do their jobs. Stephen Covey rightly points out that trustworthiness is based on both character *and* competence. People of faith cannot expect to have the most positive influence possible at work if they are not perceived as people who have both qualities. That is, they are people of character who have also paid the price exacted by hard work and continuous growth to increase in competence in their jobs.[11]

Taking this attitude toward our work requires an interior commitment every day we go to our job. That's the reason it can be called a personal discipline to be practiced.

Participate Regularly in Your Community of Faith

Do you participate in a community of faith, a congregation, a church? If so, what do you think about it? How well does it meet your needs? Whatever your answers to these questions, participating regularly in a community of faith provides important, irreplaceable resources for living faith in the world of work.

People of faith report these two seemingly conflicting evaluations of the relationship between living faith at work and participating regularly in the worship, study, fellowship, and service of one's community of faith:

• What occurs in the worship, study, fellowship, and service activities of churches appears to relate only generally if at all to what people do at work.
• People of faith who participate regularly in their congregation's activities tend to be more serious about living their faith in the workplace.

These statements may only appear to contradict each other and not actually do so. They probably indicate this: People who participate in their community of faith are more likely to think seriously about how faith applies to their lives in specific ways at work, even though their church fails to help them as pointedly as it could and should.

William E. Diehl, an active participant in his church and a former CEO, asked business executives in his denomination what they considered to be the marks of a faithful Christian business executive. Among those they considered important was commitment to participation in their church.[12]

Another study identified the strong relationship between being involved in a congregation and seeing connections between work and faith. Survey respondents were asked how separate or integrated they viewed their faith and work. The responses revealed that people who were more involved in their congregations saw more connections.[13] This same study also found that people who were more strongly grounded in the teachings of their faith tended to be more effective in relating their faith to their work.[14]

The concluding chapter of this book will provide suggestions for how congregations can be more effective in helping their members relate their faith to their work. Even without such actions on the part of congregations, however, it's still important for people of faith to participate in the activities that currently take place. Something happens in the activities of a community of faith that carries over into the lives of those who participate. Though a congregation's activities may not convey all the relevance to the real-life world of work that members need, these activities still encourage and enable people to connect their faith with their work more than would occur without participation.

If you do not feel your church is speaking to your needs, particularly your need to relate work to faith more clearly, try these suggestions:

(1) *Participate anyway.* That may be tough to do; you may feel the church is rather unconnected to your needs and thus is a waste of time and energy. I'm familiar enough with churches that in honesty I must acknowledge you may be right in too many instances. You can't try the other suggestions if you don't participate, though.

(2) *Attempt to enter into the activities with an open mind, as uncritical of what is occurring as possible.* Put yourself into these activities, and get what you can out of them in accord with the way church leadership has designed them.

(3) *Be subversive, but keep it to yourself.* Set your own agenda for every congregational event in which you participate, even though a different official agenda already exists. (This approach works at work, too, in meetings and seminars.) The fact is, you're already doing this. You might as well be honest with yourself about it and do it consciously and intentionally. Look for how what is said and done relates to your life at work, and apply that message to yourself.

(4) *Be an agent of change, as tactfully as possible.* As you have opportunity, verbalize the need to structure congregational life so that it provides laserlike help and support for people in their working lives. You may think you would be a lonely voice, but my hunch is, you will soon hear other voices joining in. Listen.

The Next Step

Get started. Max DePree wrote in his classic book on leadership, "We cannot become what we need to be by remaining what we are."[15] Practicing these personal disciplines will help you along on your pilgrimage toward becoming what you need to be as a person of faith at work.

Notes

[1]Wade Clark Roof, *A Generation of Seekers: The Spiritual Journeys of the Baby Boom Generation* (San Francisco: HarperSanFrancisco, 1993) 131.

[2]Helmut Thielicke, *The Waiting Father,* trans. with an introduction by John W. Doberstein (New York: Harper & Row, 1959) 89.

[3]Elton Trueblood, *Your Other Vocation* (New York: Harper & Brothers, 1952) 69.

[4]Philip B. Crosby, *Running Things: The Art of Making Things Happen* (New York: New American Library, 1986) 85.

[5]Karl Albrecht, *Brain Power: Learn to Improve Your Thinking Skills* (Englewood Cliffs NJ: Prentice-Hall, 1980) 34.

[6]See Thomas S. Kuhn, *The Structure of Scientific Revolutions,* 2nd ed., enlarged (Chicago: University of Chicago Press, 1970) 23.

[7]Juliet B. Schor, *The Overworked American: The Unexpected Decline of Leisure* (New York: Basic Books, 1991) 2.

[8]Alan Thein Durning, "Are We Happy Yet?" *The Futurist* (January-February 1993): 21.

[9]Dietrich Bonhoeffer, *The Cost of Discipleship* (New York: Macmillan, 1963) 194.

[10]Richard J. Foster, *Money, Sex, & Power: The Challenge of the Disciplined Life* (San Francisco: Harper & Row, 1985) 55.

[11]Stephen R. Covey, *Principle-Centered Leadership* (New York: Simon & Schuster, 1991) 31.

[12]William Diehl, *In Search of Faithfulness: Lessons from the Christian Community* (Philadelphia: Fortress Press, 1987) 31. The business executives also mentioned these: commitment to personal growth, including Bible study; an active prayer life; stewardship of money and of creation; commitment to justice; commitment to a simple lifestyle; sense of call.

[13]Stephen Hart and David A. Krueger, *Faith and Work: Personal Needs and Congregational Responses,* The Center for Ethics and Corporate Policy's

Congregations and Business Life Project, final report (Chicago: The Center for Ethics and Corporate Policy, 1991) 13-14.

[14]Stephen Hart and David Krueger, "Faith and Work: Challenges for Congregations," *The Christian Century* (15-22 July 1992): 685-86.

[15]Max DePree, *Leadership Is an Art* (New York: Doubleday, 1989) 87.

Chapter 11
How Churches Can Help

Seven of us from various parts of the city and various occupations met for an informal lunch high atop one of the city's skyscrapers. We were there, however, not to take in the view—which was impressive—or to enjoy the meal—which was good. Rather, we were there—laypeople and church professionals alike—to share our concerns about the need for churches to help their members live their faith where they spend so much of their lives: work.

One by one, people shared their pilgrimage of faith and seemed glad and a little surprised to find that they were not journeying alone as they had felt they were. Rather, at least six others, and many more whom each of us knew about, had struggled with the same concern: how churches could do a better job helping their members live their faith at work.

Now the time had come to think about what we wanted to happen. If church members actually lived their faith at work and churches actually did an effective job in preparing them to do so, what would all of this look like? If the video camera were filming what went on at work, what would people of faith be doing as they lived their faith where they worked? What actions would they be taking to demonstrate their faith? Furthermore, what would the churches be doing to prepare them to do so?

I've attempted in the previous chapters of this book to provide some guidance toward identifying what people who live their faith at work might look like—what they would do and how they would be. In this chapter I suggest some things I believe churches would look like if they were doing the most effective job of preparing their people for living their faith in the world of work. Here are eleven ways churches can take action to help their members—women as well as men, don't forget—live their faith in the world of work. These eleven ways offer sketches of possibilities, some of which some churches already have put into practice.

If churches were preparing their people for living their faith in the world of work, churches would . . .

Acknowledge the Problem and Its Seriousness

When researchers undertook a study of how Christians related to the world of work, they looked at the programs and materials, including religious education materials, of many church groups. What they found was a great scarcity of materials and a lack of concern in this area.[1] My personal acquaintance with church programs and with religious curriculum materials as a pastor, writer, editor, curriculum planner, and participant supports this conclusion.

Another leader in this area tells of having met with a group on the topic of linking faith and work. He asked them to suggest one way their pastor had helped them in this area. He gave them two weeks to think about it. Only one out of twenty-seven could name even one way! He broadened it to include fellow church members. Only two out of the twenty-seven could name anyone. They did not blame their pastor or their church. They rather simply came to realize that they themselves had focused very little on the matter of living faith in the world of work.[2]

An advertisement for a multivolume set of sermons just crossed my desk. Each volume deals with a different subject, with almost twenty volumes listed. All sorts of subjects of sermons are included— prayer, worship, suffering, hope, family, and many others. Guess what's missing? A clue: it's where people spend a third of their lives. One reason there's not a volume of sermons on the subject of work is that there wouldn't be enough of them to fill a pamphlet, much less a book, up to now.

In study sessions I have led, I have found people grateful and enthusiastic about the opportunity to deal with this area, however. One woman, a nurse, said she could not remember a time when she had had an opportunity in the church setting to talk about her Christian ministry at work as well as the frustrations of living faith at work.

In general, laypeople tend to have that attitude, while professional church leadership tend not to quite understand what all the fuss is about and why the matter is of such importance. A professional church leader said to me, not critically but with concern, when he participated in my seminar and heard what must have seemed to him like a doomsday message. "If it's as bad as all that, I'm troubled about what we've been doing in the church." I wanted to say in response: "Hooray!"

The first step toward fixing the problem is to admit that it exists and is more serious than professional church leaders imagine. Professional ministers tend to be, understandably but erroneously, most concerned about keeping the programs of the institutional church going, however much they may talk about the "ministry of the laity." They would do well to keep track of how often and how pointedly their words and actions, including the programs they promote, speak with directness to life in the working world and encourage laypeople to live out their faith there rather than on the church's property.

Laypeople involved in the world of work who cannot see the seriousness of the problem might well consider themselves fortunate indeed. They might also do well to consider undertaking a little investigation of their own to determine whether they have an especially helpful church and a great place to work or simply have developed a set of blinders that keeps them from seeing the difficulties.

With regularity, churches recognize the skills of laypeople only when churches need to "use" these "worldly" skills in the church's institutional service. For example, the schoolteacher is needed to teach church school; the banker or accountant is enlisted as the church treasurer. This use of members' skills is not necessarily bad; it's just not enough. At the same time as these churches seek out and use their members' skills for the church's institutional life, these churches rarely affirm these same people for using their skills as people of faith in the workplace. Further, churches seldom prepare these same people to live out their faith as they exercise their skills on the job.

So what happens? Church members see the institutional church as having less and less relevance for their lives. A tragic byproduct of the churches' neglect to help people connect their work with their faith is that many workers then reason that work and faith have no connection. Indeed, workers may see a contradiction between what goes on at church and what goes on at work. The result is, while work must go on, church need not go on, not for them at any rate.

Even if people continue to participate in church activities, even on a fairly regular basis, the church's calls for actions—whether these actions involve traditionally "liberal" or traditionally "conservative" tasks—tend to be ignored. Why bother to get very excited about somebody else's goals when the church is not very concerned about my own needs where I spend a third of my life—at work? People may be reluctant to voice these concerns. After all, who's listening? But they act on them weekly, demonstrating by their uninvolvement or passive involvement their feelings about a church that is uninvolved with them.

Find the True Center of the Church's Universe

Nicolaus Copernicus (1473–1543) was a Polish astronomer who came up with an unusual theory for his day. Everybody in the Western world except Copernicus followed the theory of a man named Ptolemy, who had lived 1400 years earlier. Ptolemy said that the earth was the center of the universe and that the earth did not move. Rather, all the heavenly bodies revolved around the earth. That's what it looked like to Copernicus's contemporaries when they looked at the sky.

Copernicus doubted this theory, however. He said instead that the earth was *not* the center of the universe and that the earth *did* move. A hundred or so years later, Galileo demonstrated the truth of Copernicus's ideas. Copernicus was deceased by the time Galileo got into serious trouble, which resulted in Copernicus's book being banned for 200 years. (Maybe the controvery caused sales to shoot up after that; I'm not sure.) If an author's work is going to get him into trouble, most authors would prefer it to happen 200 years after they've passed from the scene, of course! The down side is the royalties are delayed past the time they're of much use!

The point is, this same kind of refocusing of the church's view of the center of the universe needs to take place today. Churches—mainly professional ministers of the church—tend to think the center of the church's universe is the church's property and the church's activities. Such thinking is natural, understandable, inaccurate, and deadening.

As we saw in an earlier chapter, the place to which people of faith have been sent to minister is the world, not merely the church. Elton Trueblood's words are as true now as when he wrote them nearly forty-five years ago: "The message is that the world is one, secular and sacred, and that the chief way to serve the Lord is in our daily work."[3]

Do you know how the course of a large oceangoing vessel is changed? Of course, it's changed by turning the wheel that turns the rudder. But the wheel doesn't actually, directly, turn the rudder itself. What does? It's one little part of the rudder called the trim tab. The trim tab actually turns the rudder, and the rudder turns the ship.

This particular step, focusing the life of the church on what happens beyond the church walls rather than on what happens within them, functions as the trim tab for changing how the church helps people relate to the world of work. The new, true center of the church's universe must be the world, not the church, the church building, or church activities. And a large part of that world is the world of work.

Recognize Members' Ministry in the World of Work

A woman studied at a fine seminary and then served in several positions that many people would readily call "ministry." She then began to work, however, for the federal government as a crisis negotiator in civil rights problems. She also served faithfully and well in leadership positions in her church. Which would you and your church refer to as ministry—her former fulltime positions with the church, her current volunteer positions with the church, or her work with the federal government? My friend referred to her work with the federal government as the greatest opportunity for ministry she had ever had.

A young doctor became concerned about the difference in the kind of medical care that inner-city residents on welfare received and that which paying customers in nicer hospitals received. He became concerned enough, out of Christian motivations, to decide to work in the inner-city hospital, although the pay was considerably less than what he might have expected to receive. Making ends meet financially was not easy, especially with a family of college-bound children.

The young doctor believed he made the right choice. His church, however, did not recognize that the work setting he had chosen was in any way related to ministry. If he had gone to a hospital in Africa to perform the same kind of service, his church likely would have recognized him and supported him in many ways, perhaps even including financial support. Instead, his church seemed a bit concerned that it could not get the doctor to minister in his church—meaning, *in* his church building in institutional organizations.[4]

Was the young doctor's work rightly called ministry? How should the church have responded to him and his actions?

Or consider a church member who is highly respected at his place of work. In fact, he is known as the catalyst who makes things happen for good in his division. Interestingly, few people at his metropolitan church even know where and how he spends his days, much less the good he does there, even though many of his coworkers would not hesitate to apply the word "ministry" to what he does.

Similar stories of people who see their work as ministry could be multiplied. What interest does the church have in knowing about them and recognizing the ministry that occurs? Much. If the church is truly to focus on the true center of its universe, then it must identify and recognize people who model ministry in the world of work already.

A saying in business is that only what is inspected—and rewarded—gets done. Today, the church's rhetoric may encourage defining ministry as taking place beyond the church's walls—in the office, the factory, the community, the home. In reality, however, the church tends to recognize and praise participation in church activities.

People of faith who already have found opportunity for ministry in their work are doing so not to be thanked or recognized, of course. Still, a little recognition and encouragement would help, and it would heighten the visibility of such actions so that others would follow the example. But how? Here are some possibilities for churches:

- Members could be given opportunity to share with their church, or a small group within their church, what they do for a living, how it helps people, and how they see their occupation as an opportunity for ministry.
- This sharing could take place orally as well as in the church bulletins.
- The ministry opportunities members have could be recognized in worship settings, through litanies and prayers.
- Whenever "ministry" is mentioned by church leaders, the language used should include the ministry that takes place beyond the church walls, including ministry at work.

Provide Study Opportunities on Relating Faith and Work

Study opportunities on relating faith and work can aid church members in thinking about and clarifying how their faith applies to their work. Appropriate ways of providing such study opportunities include elective study sessions on this topic, special studies in retreat settings, and emphasis on this topic in the ongoing religious education program of the church.[5] Such study opportunities should involve not merely the presentation of intellectual content about the subject but, more important, time for hearing the stories of how the people in the study group struggle with living out their faith in the world of work.[6]

Develop Vocational Support Groups

One research project in the area of work and faith has identified support groups meeting regularly as an important vehicle for helping laypeople relate their work to their faith. Churches might consider for a special event gathering people in groups of five to ten people simply to talk about and learn about how to live the Christian faith in the world of work. These groups could be formed by vocations so as to facilitate conversation specifically about applying faith to that particular line of work. These vocational groups could be formed so as to continue on an ongoing basis. Another possibility is for the church to structure its existing groups so that the matter of living faith in one's vocation is addressed regularly and group members receive the support they need.

However the groups are formed, they are needed. William E. Diehl states:

> I firmly believe that if business people can be brought into Christian support groups much will happen in their faith lives. The small

group will be their linkage between Sunday faith and weekday life. I know from experience that it is true.[7]

Provide Worship Experiences
on Relating Faith to Daily Work

Mention of the challenges people face in the world of work should occur regularly in worship services. Prayers, sermons, and litanies would provide appropriate settings.

Clergy worship leaders will have to be careful that they do not make pronouncements about things they know little or nothing about, however. Many clergy will need to do a great deal more listening to the experiences of people in the world of work before they can offer more than surface help.

One way of enabling the worship leader to stay in touch authentically with these experiences is to talk with—and, more important, listen to—a representative of a given vocation during the week. The worship leader could explore the following areas with the person: (1) What are your joys in your work? (2) What are your frustrations? (3) What would you like to include in a prayer for you and others in your particular area of work?[8] A prayer or litany could then be constructed on the basis of the concerns discovered.

A church might also consider asking people to attend a worship service dressed as they do when they go to work. This would also be a test of whether the church truly shows no partiality as James 2 commands or is maintaining a social caste system based on work status. Americans are heavily influenced by social class, with the kind of work one does being a major determinant of social class. This worship service would also provide an excellent opportunity for commissioning these members to ministry in their vocational settings.

According to a recent study, work is among the subjects that sermons are least likely to address. Yet most members of congregations wish that sermons would address the subject more often. Moreover, the members' satisfaction with their congregation was greater when sermons addressed workplace issues.[9]

Teach Diligently the Basics of the Faith

Good news! One study found that people who were more strongly grounded in the teachings of their faith tended to be more effective in relating their faith to their work.[10] This finding reaffirms the importance of the church's teaching task.

Provide Career Counseling and Employment Assistance

Many churches need to be more proactive in showing a concern for members' welfare. They thus need to demonstrate more concern for their members' work life as well as their family life and their individual spiritual life. Career counseling and employment assistance are services that would offer significant help to members in these days of job uncertainty. Professionals in these areas could provide this service as a portion of their ministry.

Plan and Schedule Church Programs Sensitively

Most church participants face a myriad of demands on their time. Commuting to and from work in metropolitan areas can easily run to two hours per day. Companies are calling for extensions of work time for many salaried workers and overtime for nonsalaried ones.

Harriett, wife of Ozzie, isn't at home anymore; Harriett has a job, too. Further, the "Bill Cosby Show," depicting an upper middle class, two-career family with endless amounts of time at home, is available only in reruns. Families and individuals are harried and hurried.

Every demand has to prove its worth these days, and that includes the demands of church programs. If churches are to attract participants to church programs and activities, church leaders must make certain of the following:

• Every church program is carefully planned and presented.
• Activities are carefully prioritized and made to justify their existence.
• Activities are scheduled at times when people are available to attend them—especially activities for women, since between 55 and 60 percent of them now work outside the home.
• Guilt is not heaped on people for not attending activities that are not truly designed for them.
• Trust is extended to members as they make choices and set priorities for their participation.

Advocate a Humanized Workplace

A survey by Barciauskas and Hull revealed basically two attitudes about how dual-career or single-parent families should approach the adjustments needed in the world of work. Some suggested that making the needed adjustments was up to the individual, while others suggested that workplaces themselves should adjust.[11] The truth is, it probably is both-and, not either-or. If churches do not advocate changes, they should at least raise the issue so that decision makers in their congregations will be challenged to think about it.

One ministry that CEOs, managers, and business owners in the church could perform is to bring their faith into policy matters at their companies by advocating company policies that would humanize the workplace. Many business leaders believe that humanizing the workplace is not merely good faith but good business, in fact.

Too, people need information about how government can affect the welfare of families negatively and positively. Churches can provide this information and encourage consideration of it without engaging in partisan politics.

Some may wonder, where is the justification for the church's using this approach of advocacy? Read the little book of Philemon in the New Testament where Paul advocates freedom for a runaway slave named Onesimus.

Develop Approaches for Listening

A researcher on the effects of technology on the world of work said she learned through her research that people have a lot to say about their work, but that few people are willing to listen.[12] That unwillingness to listen extends to the church, too. The church, however, might have a more ready audience for its message if it were more willing to show that it cared about the audience by first listening to them.

There is some indication, too, that allowing people to tell their stories about something they are doing, some skill they have, some technique they use, enables them to get better at it. Living faith in the world of work fits in this category. People will get better at it when they have a chance to talk about it with fellow pilgrims on the journey.

In fact, providing opportunities to listen to people of faith tell their stories may well be the most important thing churches can do to help them. Listening is the beginning point for whatever other approaches the church decides to employ. And now it's time to get to work, *with* our faith.

Notes

[1]Stephen Hart and David A. Krueger, *Faith and Work: Personal Needs and Congregational Responses,* The Center for Ethics and Corporate Policy's Congregations and Business Life Project, final report (Chicago: The Center for Ethics and Corporate Policy, 1991) 3.

[2]Robert E. Reber, *Linking Faith & Daily Life: An Educational Program for Laypeople* (Washington DC: The Alban Institute, 1991) 161.

[3]Elton Trueblood, *The Common Ventures of Life* (New York: Harper & Brothers, 1949) 87.

[4]William E. Diehl, *Christianity and Real Life* (Philadelphia: Fortress Press, 1976) 6-9.

[5]A leader's guide for a group study of this book is available from Ross West (100 Martha Dr., Rome GA 30165-4138). Cost is $3.75.

[6]For ideas about what congregations can do in this area, see the following excellent new resource: William E. Diehl, *Ministry in Daily Life: A Practical Guide for Congregations* (Bethesda MD: The Alban Institute, 1996). For additional resource materials, see *Working: Making a Difference in God's World,* Carol Weiser, ed. (Minneapolis MN: Augsburg Fortress, 1995).

[7]William E. Diehl, *In Search of Faithfulness: Lessons from the Christian Community* (Philadelphia: Fortress Press, 1987) 74.

[8]The Colchester Federated Church, Colchester CT, uses this approach, with a committee interviewing the person during the week. The person also displays an article related to and representative of his or her work during the worship service. See Davida Foy Crabtree's excellent book about this church's work, *The Empowering Church: How One Congregation Supports Lay People's Ministries in the World* (Bethesda MD: The Alban Institute, 1989).

[9]David A. Krueger, *Keeping Faith at Work: The Christian in the Workplace* (Nashville TN: Abingdon Press, 1994) 130.

[10]Stephen Hart and David Krueger, "Faith and Work: Challenges for Congregations," *The Christian Century* (15-22 July 1992): 685-86.

[11]Rosemary Curran Barciauskas and Debra Beery Hull, *Loving and Working: Reweaving Women's Public and Private Lives* (Bloomington IN: Meyer-Stone Books, 1989) 46.

[12]Shoshana Zuboff, *In the Age of the Smart Machine: The Future of Work and Power* (New York: Basic Books, 1988) 428.

Conclusion

The difficulty with any ethics text is that one can never deal with all the issues. Life will always spring surprises. No minister can ever be fully prepared for all the situations he or she will encounter in parish life. Part of the intent of this book has been to suggest something of the range of issues a minister must deal with in entering into the professional practice of Christian ministry.

The larger purpose, however, has been to suggest by example a way of proceeding in making ethical decisions in ministry. This methodology will be seen by some people as a straight-line approach to ethical decisions. (You do this, and then you do this, and so on.) Others may prefer to think of it in terms of a complex of bases that should be touched, though not necessarily in a fixed order.

The concept itself is simple and can be practiced by those without extensive training in philosophical or ethical inquiry. Every Christian decision is assumed to be a decision with an authority base somewhere in Christian teaching. The minister's task is to seek to locate the appropriate authority base for each issue and bring it to bear as he or she makes decisions. As a conservative Christian (on the grand scale of things), I have chosen to locate my basis of authority in the Bible. Therefore, each ministry ethics decision is made in some fashion as follows.

One begins with trying to understand the question. What issue must be decided? How has that issue been dealt with in church history as a whole and in one's own particular denominational, cultural, and ministerial context? What insights do secular history and social sciences have to offer?

Once the issue is clearly defined, and all relevant facts are in hand, one moves to examine possible sources of authority. How have other ministers responded? What about Christian ethicists? What biblical principles inform the situation or decision called for?

Since biblical principles are paramount for me, these alone may sometimes determine much of the shape of a particular response. For the Christian, however, there is also always the more mystical element of the impetus of the Holy Spirit. One assumes that, given time, a Christian minister will pray about ministry decisions and seek the guidance of the Holy Spirit in making them.

Finally, however, one must decide a course of action, plan it, and carry it out. This course of action may then be altered as experience teaches. The minister who never alters an ethical choice on the basis of experience and feedback simply is not paying attention.

This ethical method is essentially that taught by Henlee Barnette for many years at the Southern Baptist Theological Seminary. Its great advantage lies in its accessibility to thoughtful Christians with or without extensive ethical training. Other methods are more sophisticated, but this one can shed light on virtually any significant ethical issue if carefully applied.

Select Bibliography

Austin, Nancy. Ethics: "Personal vs. Professional." *Working Woman* (September 1992): 28, 32.

Autry, James A. *Love and Profit: The Art of Caring Leadership.* New York: William Morrow & Co., 1991.

Life and Work: A Manager's Search for Meaning. New York: William Morrow & Co., 1994.

Banks, Robert J., compiler. *Faith Goes to Work: Reflections from the Marketplace.* Washington DC: The Alban Institute, 1993.

Barciauskas, Rosemary Curran and Debra Beery Hull. *Loving and Working: Reweaving Women's Public and Private Lives.* Bloomington IN: Meyer-Stone Books, 1989.

Barnette, Henlee. *Has God Called You?* Nashville TN: Broadman Press, 1969.

Bellah, Robert N. et al. *Habits of the Heart: Individualism and Commitment in American Life.* Berkeley CA: University of California Press, 1985.

Bertram, Georg. "ergon." *The Theological Dictionary of the New Testament.* 2: 635-52. Edited by Gerhard Kittel. Translated and edited by Geoffrey W. Bromiley. Grand Rapids MI: Eerdmans, 1964.

Boggs, Wade H., Jr. *All Ye Who Labor: A Christian Interpretation of Daily Work.* Richmond VA: John Knox Press, 1961.

Bolles, Richard Nelson. *What Color Is Your Parachute? A Practical Manual for Job-Hunters & Career-Changers.* Berkeley CA: Ten Speed Press, 1996.

Booher, Dianna. *First Thing Monday Morning.* Old Tappan NJ: Fleming H. Revell, 1988.

_____. *First Thing Monday Morning: Weekly Meditations for Your Work Week.* Nashville TN: Thomas Nelson, 1993.

Broholm, Dick, and John Hoffman. Editing and revision by Janet Madore. *Empowering Laity for Their Full Ministry.* Newton MA: Andover-Newton Center for the Ministry of the Laity, 1982.

Burkett, Larry. *Business by the Book: The Complete Guide of Biblical Principles for Business Men and Women.* Nashville TN: Thomas Nelson, 1990.

Calhoun, Robert Lowry. *God and the Day's Work: Christian Vocation in an Unchristian World.* New York: Association Press, 1957.

Campbell, Dennis M. Doctors, *Lawyers, Ministers: Christian Ethics in Professional Practice.* Nashville TN: Abingdon, 1982.

Chappell, Tom. *The Soul of a Business: Managing for Profit and the Common Good.* New York: Bantam Books, 1993.

Covey, Stephen R. *The Seven Habits of Highly Effective People: Restoring the Character Ethic.* New York: Simon & Schuster, 1989.

_____. *Principle-Centered Leadership.* New York: Simon & Schuster, 1991.

Cowan, John. *Small Decencies: Reflections and Meditations on Being Human at Work.* New York: HarperBusiness, 1992.

_____. *The Common Table: Reflections and Meditations on Community and Spirituality in the Workplace.* New York: HarperBusiness, 1993.

Crabtree, Davida Foy. *The Empowering Church.* Washington DC: The Alban Institute, 1989.

DePree, Max. *Leadership Is an Art.* New York: Doubleday, 1989.

_____. *Leadership Jazz.* New York: Dell Publishing, 1992.

Diehl, William E. *Christianity and Real Life.* Philadelphia: Fortress Press, 1976.

_____. *In Search of Faithfulness: Lessons from the Christian Community.* Philadelphia: Fortress Press, 1987.

_____. *Thank God, Its Monday!* Laity Exchange Books. Philadelphia: Fortress Press, 1982.

_____. *Ministry in Daily Life: A Practical Guide for Congregations.* Bethesda MD: The Alban Institute, 1996.

_____. *Higher Than the Highest.* Reprinted from Guideposts, 1952 1992. Nashville TN: Dimensions for Living, 1993.

Dosick, Wayne. *The Business Bible: Ten New Commandments for Creating an Ethical Workplace.* New York: William Morrow, 1993.

Douglass, Merrill E., and Donna N. *Manage Your Time, Your Work, Yourself.* Updated edition. New York: AMACOM, 1993.

Edelman, Marian Wright. *The Measure of Our Success: A Letter to My Children and Yours.* New York: HarperPerennial, 1992.

Edge, Findley. *The Greening of the Church.* Waco TX: Word, 1971.

Fowler, James. *Becoming Adult, Becoming Christian: Adult Development and Christian Faith.* New York: HarperCollins, 1984.

Fox, Matthew. *The Reinvention of Work: A New Vision of Livelihood for Our Time.* San Francisco: HarperSanFrancisco, 1994.

Geoghegan, Thomas. *Which Side Are You On? Trying to Be for Labor When It's Flat on Its Back.* New York: Penguin Books, 1991.

Greenleaf, Robert K. *Servant Leadership: A Journey into the Nature of Legitimate Power and Greatness.* New York: Paulist Press, 1977.

Hall, William D. *Making the Right Decision: Ethics for Managers.* New York: John Wiley & Sons, Inc., 1993.

Hart, Stephen, and David A. Krueger. *Faith and Work: Personal Needs and Congregational Responses.* The Center for Ethics and Corporate Policy's Congregations and Business Life Project. Final report. Chicago IL: The Center for Ethics and Corporate Policy, 1991.

_____. "Faith and Work: Challenges for Congregations." *The Christian Century* (15-22 July 1992): 683-86.

Hauck, Friedrich. "kopos." *Theological Dictionary of the New Testament.* 3:827-30. Edited by Gerhard Kittel. Translated and edited by Geoffrey W. Bromiley. Grand Rapids MI: Eerdmans, 1965.

Haughey, John C. *Converting Nine to Five: A Spirituality of Daily Work.* New York: Crossroad, 1989.

Hybels, Bill. *Christians in the Marketplace.* Wheaton IL: Victor Books, 1982.

Jarman, W. Maxey. *A Businessman Looks at the Bible.* Westwood NJ: Fleming H. Revell, 1965.

Jones, Laurie Beth. *Jesus, CEO: Using Ancient Wisdom for Visionary Leadership.* New York: Hyperion, 1995.

Kimmel, Michael S. "What Do Men Want?" *Harvard Business Review* (November–December 1993): 50-63.

Kohn, Alfie. *No Contest: The Case Against Competition.* Revised edition. Boston: Houghton Mifflin, 1992.

Krueger, David A. "Connecting Ministry with the Corporate World." *The Christian Century* (30 May 6 June 1990): 572-74.

_____. *Keeping Faith at Work: The Christian in the Workplace.* Nashville TN: Abingdon, 1992.

Liebig, James E. *Business Ethics: Profiles in Civic Virtue.* Golden CO: Fulcrum Publishing, 1990.

McKenna, David L. *Love Your Work!* Wheaton IL: Victor Books,1990.

McMakin, Jacqueline, with Sonya Dyer. *Working from the Heart.* San Diego CA: LuraMedia, 1989.

Mead, Loren B. *The Once and Future Church: Reinventing the Congregation for a New Mission Frontier.* Washington DC: The Alban Institute, 1991.

Menking, Stanley L., and Barbara Wendlund. *God's Partners: Lay Christians at Work.* Valley Forge PA: Judson Press, 1993.

Merton, Thomas. *Life and Holiness.* New York: Doubleday, 1963.

Middleton, Robert G. "Revising the Concept of Vocation for the Industrial Age." *The Christian Century* (29 October 1986): 943- 45.

Miller, Alexander. *Christian Faith and My Job.* New York: Association Press, 1946.

Miller, Keith. *The Taste of New Wine.* Waco TX: Word, 1965.

Million, Elmer G. *Your Faith and Your Life Work.* New York: Friendship Press, 1960.

Moore, Thomas. *Care of the Soul: A Guide for Cultivating Depth and Sacredness in Everyday Life.* New York: HarperCollins, 1992.

Nash, Laura L. *Good Intentions Aside: A Manager's Guide to Resolving Ethical Problems.* Boston: Harvard Business School Press, 1990.

_____. *Believers in Business.* Nashville TN: Thomas Nelson, 1994.

Naylor, Thomas H. "Redefining Corporate Motivation, Swedish Style." *The Christian Century* (30 May–6 June 1990): 566-70.

Nelson, John Oliver, editor. *Work and Vocation: A Christian Discussion.* New York: Harper & Brothers, 1954.

Nelson, Martha. *The Christian Woman in the Working World.* Nashville TN: Broadman Press, 1970.

Niebuhr, H. Richard. *Christ and Culture.* New York: Harper & Row, 1951.

Oates, Wayne E. *Convictions That Give You Confidence. Potentials: Guides for Productive Living.* Philadelphia: Westminster Press, 1984.

Raines, John C., and Donna C. Day-Lower. *Modern Work and Human Meaning.* Philadelphia: Westminster Press, 1986.

Reber, Robert E. *Linking Faith & Daily Life: An Educational Program for Lay People.* Washington DC: The Alban Institute, 1991.

Reeck, Darrell. *Ethics for the Professions: A Christian Perspective.* Minneapolis: Augsburg, 1982.

Richardson, Alan. *The Biblical Doctrine of Work.* London: SCM, 1963.

Rush, Myron. *Lord of the Marketplace.* Wheaton IL: Victor Books, 1986.

Schmidt, K. L. "kaleo," "klasis." *The Theological Dictionary of the New Testament.* 3:487-93. Edited by Gerhard Kittel. Translated and edited by Geoffrey W. Bromiley. Grand Rapids MI: Eerdmans, 1965.

Schumacher, Ernst Friendrich. *Good Work.* New York: Harper & Row, 1979.

Segler, Franklin M. *The Christian Layman.* Nashville TN: Broadman Press, 1964.

Sheldon, Charles M. *In His Steps.* Nashville TN: Broadman Press, 1973.

Shelly, Judith Allen. *Not Just a Job: Serving Christ in Your Work.* Downers Grove IL: InterVarsity Press, 1985.

Sherman, Doug, and William Hendricks. *Your Work Matters to God.* Colorado Springs CO: NavPress, 1987.

Soelle, Dorothee, with Shirley A. Cloyes. *To Work and to Love.* Philadelphia: Fortress Press, 1984.

Teilhard de Chardin, Pierre. *The Divine Milieu: An Essay on the Interior Life.* New York: Harper & Row, 1960.

Trueblood, Elton. *The Common Ventures of Life.* New York: Harper & Brothers, 1949.

_____. *Your Other Vocation.* New York: Harper & Brothers, 1952.

Tuleja, Tad. *Beyond the Bottom Line: How Business Leaders Are Turning Principles into Profits.* New York: Facts on File Publications, 1985.

Volf, Miroslav. *Work in the Spirit: Toward a Theology of Work.* New York: Oxford University Press, 1991.

Weiser, Carol, ed. *Working: Making a Difference in God's World.* Minneapolis: Augsburg Fortress, 1995.

West, Ross. *How to Be Happier in the Job You Sometimes Can't Stand.* Nashville TN: Broadman Books, 1990; paperback, New York: Warner Books, 1992.

Williams, A. L. *All You Can Do Is All You Can Do, But All You Can Do Is Enough.* Nashville TN: Oliver-Nelson Books,1988.

Wolf, C. U. Labor. *The Interpreter's Dictionary of the Bible.* 3:51-52. New York: Abingdon, 1962.

_____. "Occupations." *The Interpreter's Dictionary of the Bible.* 3:589. New York: Abingdon, 1962.

_____. "Servant." *The Interpreter's Dictionary of the Bible.* 3:291-92. New York: Abingdon, 1962.

Wuthnow, Robert. *God and Mammon in America.* New York: The Free Press, 1994.

Zuboff, Shoshana. *In the Age of the Smart Machine: The Future of Work and Power.* New York: Basic Books, 1988.

About the Author

Ross West writes, speaks, leads seminars, and provides consulting services for businesses and churches. He also provides assistance and consulting in writing, editing, and publishing. In addition, he is a founder and coordinator of an organization that assists churches in providing quality Christian education.

His career has contained considerably more variation than he could have imagined several years ago. In addition to a student pastorate in Kentucky, he served as a pastor of churches in Arkansas, Virginia, and Louisiana. Next, he became an editor and then an editorial section manager at the Baptist Sunday School Board in Nashville, Tennessee, where he worked for years. He then served as Director of Creative Services for the Boy Scouts of America, Irving, Texas.

He holds degrees from New Orleans Baptist Theological Seminary, Southern Baptist Theological Seminary, and Louisiana Tech University. His wife, Martha, teaches at Shorter College, Rome, Georgia. They have a son, a daughter-in-law, and two grandchildren.

In addition to sermons and seminars on faith in the workplace, Ross West provides presentations for business on such topics as coping with stress, mastering time management, how to be happier in the job you sometimes can't stand, developing ethical people in an ethical organization, developing managers who lead people, measuring and increasing customer satisfaction, and writing for business. For assistance for your church, business, or other organization, you may contact him at the address below.

Are you thinking of using this book as the basis for a group study in your church, at a retreat, or with an informal group in your workplace? A leader's guide for a group study of this book is available by writing Ross West and enclosing a check for $4.75.

Do you have a story to tell about how you live your faith in the workplace? or about how someone you respect does? or about how a church is preparing its members to live their faith in the workplace? You're invited to share the news with Ross West at the address provided. Perhaps your story can provide encouragement to others.

Ross West
Positive Difference Communications
100 Martha Drive
Rome, GA 30165-4138
706-232-9325 (Phone) 706-235-2716 (Fax)